AF405906

Stories

for

Young Minds

that

Really

like to

Think

An Introduction to
Philosophy for Kids

Victoria Barker

Copyright © 2022 Victoria Barker

All rights reserved

STORIES FOR YOUNG MINDS THAT REALLY LIKE TO THINK
AN INTRODUCTION TO PHILOSOPHY FOR KIDS

FOR

ANTONIA

AND

SEBASTIAN

WITH MY

LOVE

Preface

This book is a collection of stories which raise questions of philosophical interest. You might well ask: what does that mean? How can a story raise questions of philosophical interest? And what exactly is a question of philosophical interest?

There are many traditions of philosophy across the globe, each with its own specialised interests and techniques. Within Anglo-American thought, the primary focus of this volume, there are two senses in which the word 'philosophy' tends to be used.

The first is used when someone says, 'It is my philosophy that we should respect the religious beliefs of others' or asks, 'What is your philosophy on eating meat?' Here the word is used to refer to a worldview, a view that has benefitted from considered thought and provides the basis for reasoned behaviour.

The second is used when we talk about the philosophy of Aristotle or the philosophy of art or the philosophy of existentialism. Here the word is used to refer to an academic discipline, a tradition of thought about a fairly specialised set of questions. Often, these questions take the form, 'What is …?': What is truth? What is goodness? What is art?

A story is told about the British philosopher GE Moore, who when asked, 'What is philosophy?' gestured in the direction of his bookshelves and replied, 'It is the stuff in those books.' He was using the word in this second sense.

In this collection, I will introduce the second of these uses of the word 'philosophy', referring to arguments and theories that have been presented through the course of the tradition of Western philosophy by a wide range of philosophers on a wide range of topics. For the most part, however, the questions raised, while of philosophical interest, are not raised by these philosophers themselves, but by stories of folklore or classical literature or stories of more recent origin that are designed primarily to entertain rather than to teach.

These stories have been chosen because they are inspired by ideas that are the stuff of philosophical debate. And this in turn suggests that, while philosophy may be a discipline of thought within academic institutions, it is not limited to these institutions. The ideas of philosophy are found in literature, in art, in film, in the sciences and indeed across the entirety of our culture. Thus the second definition of philosophy points in the direction of the first.

More importantly, philosophy is something we engage in ourselves when we ask such basic questions as, 'How do I know that what I believe is true?' or 'Why should I do the right thing?' These are questions which all of us should ask ourselves from time to time and so it is interesting to consider how some of the great minds of our philosophical traditions have chosen to address them.

CHAPTER ONE

AN ELF'S TREASURE

There was once a student who lived in a garret perched on the top of a merchant's house. The student was poor – as students sometimes are – having spent many years studying the greatest treasures of literature at the University of Copenhagen. Yet, despite the lack of pennies tumbling in his pocket, he was happy and cheerful. He knew little of the cares of the world.

On the ground floor of the house, underneath the student's garret, was a shop, where the merchant and his wife sold groceries and delicacies of every description – though, needless to say, the student could afford little of what the merchant had to sell. On the first and the second floors were the merchant's living rooms and at the bottom, in the cellar, were rooms for storage. It was here, in the furthest corner of a dark recess, in a pile of warm and comfortable cushions and blankets, that there lived an elf.

Now the elf was – as elves sometimes are – a grumpy soul, though no less useful to the merchant for all that. For many years, he had been a loyal servant of his master, heaving and hauling the merchant's wares up and down the stairs and around the shop. He was paid for his labours with a large bowl of porridge on Sundays, complete with a generous dollop of cream, and seemed reasonably content with that. He was proud of his work and even more proud of his trusted position in the household, as well he might be.

One evening, the student came through the back door of the shop to buy for himself a meagre supper of bread and cheese. He selected what he wanted, paid for it with his pennies, and the merchant bid him a polite farewell. The student nodded too, but then suddenly stopped short, staring at the sheet of paper in which the bread was wrapped. It appeared to be a page torn from an old book, a book that ought not to have been torn up, a book that still had a tale to tell.

The merchant watched him with amusement. 'Over there is more of the same,' he said, pointing his chin towards a pile of old books on the cutting bench. 'Give me another penny and you can take the rest of the book that has you so captivated.'

'Give me the book instead of the cheese,' replied the student, handing the cheese back to the merchant and pocketing the book before the merchant could decide otherwise. 'I can eat my bread without cheese tonight and it would be a sin to tear up the book entirely. You are a good man, a practical man, but I think you care no more for literature than that sack of potatoes over there.'

Doubtless his words could have been taken as an insult – not least to the potatoes – but the merchant laughed, because he knew that they were the truth, in so many words. Throughout this interchange, sitting quietly on a stool in a corner of the room and listening attentively, was the elf. He was not entirely pleased with the student's joke and took offense on his master's behalf. He huffed and hawed after the student retreated up the back steps, signalling his discontent to the merchant. He determined to have words with the student, to demand that he show respect where it was due.

So, when the shop door was closed and the blind pulled down, the elf made his way grumpily up the back stairs to the student's garret. Quietly, he stole up to the room and peeped through the keyhole. There indeed was the student at his desk, the crumbs of his meal scattered around him, concentrating intently on the open pages of the book he had acquired from the shop below. A single candle was burning on his desk, for these were the days before electricity lit up our houses like firecrackers.

Yet how bright was his room! Out of the open page of the book shot a clear, lustrous beam of light. The light expanded upwards, rising and reaching outwards to form the shape of a mighty tree, which grew to the ceiling and spread its branches out across the beams. The tips of the branches dropped down over the head of the reader, as if sheltering him. The leaves of the tree hung downwards in brilliant beads of illumination, which fluttered in the candlelight and bathed the reader in a glittering halo of light.

Each leaf twinkled with a gentle rustling sound, which resonated around the room, creating a chorus of tiny voices.

Never had the elf seen or heard anything like it. Never had he imagined such a thing. He stood mesmerised, following every movement of the student's eyes as he devoured the book in front of him. The elf's face mirrored that of the student, whose eyes glistened in the light as he mouthed a few of the words on the page and then smiled, pleased by what he had read. The elf stood there on tiptoe, entirely still, gazing at the student until the candle went out. Probably the student blew it out and went to bed, but the elf remained standing there nonetheless, for the music sounded on, soft and delicate, a dreamlike serenade for the student as he rested.

'This is incredible!' whispered the elf to himself, when the student was fast asleep. 'Just incredible!' he repeated. 'Is this how a student lives? How did I not know this before?'

Now the elf, like his master, was a practical soul, who knew a thing or two about the cares of the world. He knew, for example, that the student could not provide him with a large bowl of porridge on Sundays, complete with a dollop of cream. But he saw now that some things are not measured in this way and that some things were not exchanged for comforts of this nature. Now he knew that, beyond the activity of the merchant's shop, beyond the heaving and hauling, there were other activities going on in the household, activities of a different kind. These too demanded his attention. So, casting aside his earlier doubts, the elf resolved to look after the student and keep him safe.

From that night on, the elf would no longer sit quietly in his cosy corner of the cellar in the evening. As soon as the light glimmered in the garret, he felt himself drawn by tiny voices towards the keyhole. He felt obliged to peep in, to check on the student, to ensure that all was well. When he did, a feeling of greatness swept over him and tears swelled in his eyes. At those moments, he no longer felt grumpy. 'How glorious it would be to sit with the student under the tree!' he thought. It was only when the light in the room finally dimmed that he shivered and crept down to the cellar, where it was warm and comfortable and he could lie and wonder at what he had seen.

One night, the elf dreamt a wonderful dream. He dreamt that he knocked on the door of the student's garret and was welcomed into the room. He dreamt that he took a seat with the student at his desk and was engulfed by the light of the tree which rose from the book on the desk over his head. He felt the light wash over him and through him, fracturing into tiny splinters that resembled happiness and freedom and hope.

Suddenly, he was awakened from his reveries by a terrible tumult, the sound of people running and yelling outside in the street. Someone was rapping noisily on the windowpanes of the merchant's shop. The elf roused himself and went upstairs, to find the household in chaos. A great fire had broken out somewhere in the neighbourhood and the street was full of smoke and flames. Which way were the flames heading? Whose house would be consumed next?

The merchant was running around in circles, shouting at the elf to haul his possessions from the house and into the yard, where they might be saved. Meanwhile, the merchant's wife had in mind to save her own treasures and a furious argument broke out between them. The elf, naturally, felt the same way towards his own possessions. He thought of the warm, comfortable blankets in his corner of the cellar and he thought of the beloved bowl in which he was served his porridge on Sundays … but these thoughts were fleeting.

Ignoring the merchant, the elf bounded towards the back steps and was up the stairs in a few leaps, throwing open the door of the garret and looking around at the room in which he had sat in his dream only moments before. He saw the student standing quietly at his open window, staring at the conflagration raging in the houses nearby. He turned to the table and there was the book, open at the page where its reader had left it. To the student's great surprise, the elf seized the book and popped it into his red cap, which he held tightly in both hands. Sidestepping the student, the elf sprang out the window, onto the roof and across the top of the houses.

The elf ended up huddled on a chimney streets away, far from the flames. He was still clutching his cap in both hands, the book safe and sound within. There he sat, illuminated by the flames in the distance, clasping his treasure firmly to his chest. And as he sat there, a great sigh of relief escaped him, for now at last he knew the true feelings of his heart.

Later, when the fire was extinguished and the elf could think calmly, he returned to the merchant's house and found it and its inhabitants unharmed. The merchant, the merchant's wife and the student were all as they were, unchanged by the excitement of the night's events. The elf returned the book to its rightful owner and took his leave of the household. For he knew that he himself was greatly changed – excepting of course in this, that he still loved a large bowl of porridge on Sundays, complete with a generous dollop of cream.

These are the first pages of a long and curious story of how a small and humble elf became a great and prolific reader and – so it is said – came to write books of his own in time. And perhaps what the story shows is that the tree of knowledge may appear to any of us and that, sometimes, it is merely a matter of allowing ourselves to be captivated by its beauty.

What do you think?
Questions to ponder

Why did the student value his book so highly, do you think? What did he get from his reading?

Do you agree that the 'tree of knowledge' may appear to anyone – or must you be a particular type of person to see it?

If you were in an emergency and could save only one of your possessions, what would it be? Why?

PHILOSOPHICAL CONUNDRUMS: WHY STUDY IDEAS?

This is an adaptation of a story written by the Danish writer of fairy tales, Hans Christian Andersen, famous for *The Little Mermaid*, *The Ugly Duckling*, *The Emperor's New Clothes* and many other much-loved tales. I have included this as an introductory piece because of its focus on the value of literature, and of writing more generally, to our culture.

The form of writing that concerns us in this collection is the writing of the history of ideas, which we call philosophy. The word 'philosophy' comes from Ancient Greek and translates as 'the love of wisdom'. This is what I picture the elf discovering in this tale. Philosophy is an important field of writing in many cultures. Ancient Greece is also the source of the first great writings of Western philosophy, the most important of which were penned in the 4th century BC by a philosopher whose name was Plato.

So great is Plato's influence on the history of Western ideas that an English philosopher, Alfred North Whitehead, once described the tradition of philosophy as a series of 'footnotes to Plato'. He meant that the philosophical ideas that we discuss today can be traced back to Plato's writings and to the questions Plato posed – defining the scope of this field of inquiry in the process.

Whitehead's comment highlights the fact that philosophy is, first and foremost, a tradition of writing, complete with footnotes at the bottom of its pages. Philosophy is a tradition precisely because its earliest treasures were preserved, reproduced by hand in folios and books, in libraries which somehow survived wars, natural disasters and other calamities, and so made it into the modern age, to be reproduced in print and then digitally, for the benefit of all who wish to read them.

What did Plato write about, then, such that these writings should be so influential? What questions did he pose for philosophy? There are a great many, but these are typical: what is truth? Why be good? What brings happiness? What is the difference between knowledge and mere belief? What ultimately exists? These are the questions we will consider in the following pages, by way of stories that raise these questions in more or less obvious ways.

Turning back to this story, then, what questions does it raise and how are these questions of philosophy? The first and perhaps the most interesting is this: what did the student gain from the book he read so intently? We know the student enjoyed his book, since he forsook his basic needs – his food – for the pleasure of reading it. This may be enough in itself to justify the book and its ideas. But, further to this, Andersen clearly wishes us to understand that the ideas found in the book are important in themselves, are things of extraordinary value and beauty.

Now we would of course expect the student to find literary ideas important, since he has been trained specifically to see them in this way. By introducing the elf into his story, Andersen's aim, I take it, is to show that the ideas in the book are also important to others, besides scholars. Even the elf, a small and humble soul, can see for himself their value and beauty. Indeed, these ideas prove even more important to the elf than to the student, since reading the book – even if only in his dreams – leads the elf to make decisions that change his life irrevocably. Not only for the student, but also for the elf, these ideas are not merely valuable and beautiful, but transformative. Philosophers tend to look on the ideas of philosophy in this same way.

Philosophy discusses ideas which relate to a great many fields of human understanding: ideas to do with science, art, law, religion, for example. In each of these areas, there is a philosophy: a philosophy of science, a philosophy of art, and so on. Underlying these are deeper questions that underpin the discipline as a whole: what is truth, what is knowledge, what is wisdom? These are not merely questions within philosophy, but questions that determine what philosophy should be, what it should aim for and how it should be practiced. This is why questions about what philosophy is and why we should do it – why study ideas, why think philosophically? – are among the most profound philosophical questions of all.

Why think about the ideas introduced by Plato? This is a question I hope the reader will ponder through the course of this book. Various answers will suggest themselves in these pages: because it is enjoyable and fun, because it teaches skills in abstract reasoning, because it gives us tools to think more clearly on problems that challenge us, because it makes us question beliefs we normally take for granted ... There are many, many reasons besides.

Before moving on, let me draw attention to two prominent metaphors found in this story: the metaphors of the tree and the light. A metaphor is a way of describing a thing by referring to another, using a non-literal or non-standard meaning to make the description more powerful: for example, a ticking clock might be a metaphor for the passage of time, or a sunrise might be a metaphor for a new beginning. Metaphors often play a critical role in expressing ideas in literature and in philosophy. In this story, the tree can be seen as a metaphor for the knowledge in the student's book and the light can be seen as a metaphor for the enlightenment which such knowledge bestows on its reader.

These two metaphors have been popular throughout modern philosophy. In the 17th century, the French philosopher René Descartes wrote metaphorically of the whole of human knowledge as represented by a tree. The tree's roots, he wrote, represent our most certain truths, which firmly anchor everything that stands above. The trunk represents the knowledge that grows from our most certain truths, drawing nutrients from the roots below and channelling them to the tree's branches, which represent the various branches of learning of the sciences and the arts.

Our learning in these branches of knowledge gives us enlightenment, a light made possible by the 'light of reason' within us, which Descartes took to be given to us by God. Whether divine or not, the light of reason remains a powerful metaphor across our philosophical and literary traditions because it reminds us of the brilliance of the ideas which have driven our cultures and made possible their greatest achievements.

CHAPTER TWO

MISTRESS PRIDGETT'S SECOND SIGHT

Old Mistress Pridgett was a warm, good-natured and practical person, whose purpose in life was to go about nursing sick people and making them well again. She had a reputation for being good at her job. She was diligent and hard-working and widely sought after for her skills.

One Saturday, Mistress Pridgett was sitting in her rocking chair at the end of a hard week's work when, through the window, she saw a man come riding along the road at great speed on a magnificent, prancing black horse. He rode up to her door and knocked without even getting down from the horse. When Mistress Pridgett answered, he stared at her with such intense eyes, he almost frightened her.

'Are you Mistress Pridgett?' he asked.

'I am.'

'Do you go about nursing sick people?' he asked.

'I do.'

'Then you are the one I want. My wife is ill and I am looking for someone to care for her,' he said urgently.

Mistress Pridgett did not know the man, but knew that he was not a neighbour. 'Where do you live?' she asked.

'There is no time to talk. Give me your hand and get up behind me,' the man insisted.

Mistress Pridgett gave him her hand, not because she wanted to, but because somehow she felt she was unable to refuse. With the slightest tug, the man pulled her up from her doorway and onto the horse behind him. Then, on his whistle, the horse flew like the wind, so fast that all Mistress Pridgett could do was shut her eyes and hold on tight to the stranger.

They rode a great distance and then stopped before a poor, dilapidated house. Mistress Pridgett did not know where they were and she stared about her. It was a dreary place. In front of the house were rocks with weeds growing among them and a pool of muddy water. Dry, spindly plants were scattered about. She was surprised that a man with such a magnificent horse should bring her to such a drab house, but her job was to nurse a sick woman and that is what she intended to do.

They passed through a cramped hallway into a room hung around with cobwebs. The room was poorly furnished with a wooden bed, a table and chair. In the bed lay a small, shrunken woman with coarse, weathered skin. In the crook of her arm was a baby so small and fragile that Mistress Pridgett knew it could not have been more than a few hours old.

'This is my wife,' said the stranger tenderly. 'Please care for her.'

The man showed Mistress Pridgett the kitchen and she fetched a basin of water to wash the baby. But, when she bent over to lift the child from the bed, it reached out and gave her such a thump on the ear that her head rang. She was so stunned that she cried out and almost let the baby fall from her arms.

'What is the matter?' said the woman weakly. 'Is she upset?' Then the woman slipped her hand under her pillow and pulled out a jar of ointment. 'Here, rub the child's eyes with this,' she instructed. 'It will soothe her. But do not get any of it in your own eyes or it will be very, very bad.' So the nurse rubbed the ointment on the baby's eyes. Then the mother told her to be careful to wash off any of it that was left on her finger and the nurse did as she was told.

All that day and the next, Mistress Pridgett looked after the mother and child. She washed the baby and rubbed the ointment on its eyelids and again the mother warned her to be careful not to let the least bit of it touch her own eye. She was given a room and food and, although she did not know where the food came from nor who prepared it, she was happy for it all the same because she worked hard caring for the woman and her baby.

Day followed day and they were all much the same for Mistress Pridgett. She looked after the mother as best she knew how. She washed the baby and rubbed ointment on its eyelids, as she had been told. Soon the child's eyes, that had at first been dull, grew so bright and strong that they sparkled like precious jewels. Mistress Pridgett began to think that it must be a very fine ointment and that she would like to try it on her own eyes, since her eyesight was starting to grow dim with age.

Now, every day, after Mistress Pridgett had washed the baby, she left the basin on a chair beside her while she rubbed the ointment on the child's eyes. One day, she upset the basin with her elbow as though by accident, but in fact entirely by design. She let out a cry and bent over to pick up the basin. As she did so, unseen by her patient in the bed, she rubbed her left eye with the finger she had used for the baby's ointment, which still had a little of the ointment remaining on it.

When Mistress Pridgett straightened up and looked about her, she could hardly keep from crying out. The room and everything within it was utterly changed. Instead of being poor and humble, it appeared to be a chamber within a large mansion or castle. Where there had been cobwebs, there were now delicate hangings; where there had been rough blankets were beautiful soft silk coverings; where there had been simple wooden furniture were bright gilded furnishings. The woman she had been nursing was not in the least shrunken and weathered, but in fact a young woman of fine and noble bearing.

Mistress Pridgett managed somehow to stay quiet and hide her amazement, but now she knew very well that the land to which she had come was not of her own world, but belonged to the fairy folk. She made some excuse to go to the window and look out. The change outside was no less wondrous than that within. The muddy pool was now a glittering lake, the rocks were grottoes, the trees were lush and full and covered with shining fruit, and the weeds were flowers of the most extraordinary colours.

For the remainder of her visit to the young couple's household, Mistress Pridgett managed to act in such a manner that the couple never suspected she could see the truth of who they were and how they lived. But it was only with her left eye that she saw them in their true state, the eye which had been touched by the ointment. When she closed that eye and looked with the other, everything was as it had been before.

Time went on until the fairy woman was strong and well again and had no need of a nurse to take care of her. One day, her husband came on his black horse and called Mistress Pridgett out to him in the yard. 'Thank you for your kind service,' he said formally. Then he caught hold of her hand and hurled her up behind him onto the horse, which flew so quickly that, when she reached her home, she knew no more of the way she had come than she knew of the way she had gone. Whatever her confusion, it was well-compensated by the purse of gold coins she found in the pocket of her apron.

This was not the last Mistress Pridgett saw of the fairy folk. The man on the black horse came no more, but there were others about in the world who were now visible to her with her left eye. Sometimes as she came through the wood, she would see them setting their houses in order and living their quiet, comfortable lives. On moonlit nights, she would sometimes see them dancing in the meadows or on the hillside. She never told a soul about what she saw, nor tried to speak to the fairy people, and they were so busy with their own affairs that they paid no attention to her, nor guessed that she could see them.

But then at last came a day when she met the fairy woman once again. She had gone to the market to buy fabric for a new dress, which she could now well afford, thanks to her new gold coins. She was paying little attention to what was going on around her, thinking only of the fabric she was to buy, when she felt a hand in her pocket. She looked down and realised with horror that someone had taken from her pocket the coins she had brought to pay for the fabric.

Looking this way and that, she saw the back of a man striding away from her. She was certain the man had just been standing behind her and that it was he who had stolen her coins. But she saw someone else as well. Standing in the path of the thief, ready to trip him so that he dropped the coins still in his hand, was the fairy woman, who thrust out her leg just as the man approached. Since the thief had no way of knowing the fairy woman was even there, he tripped right over her leg and landed in a heap on the ground.

'Miserable thief, I'm taking back those coins you've stolen from me!' cried Mistress Pridgett indignantly, rushing to collect her coins as they fell from his hand.

As she did so, Mistress Pridgett laughed out loud at what the fairy woman had done and inadvertently caught the eye of the woman herself.

The fairy woman stopped and looked at her. 'So you can see me, can you?' said the woman smoothly, more in surprise than in anger.

'Yes, to be sure, I can,' Mistress Pridgett admitted, honest soul that she was.

'Some of the ointment touched your eye, then?' the fairy woman asked.

'Yes, it did.'

'Both eyes or just the one?'

'No, just the left one,' Mistress Pridgett replied.

The woman leaned forwards, as if she wished to stare deep into Mistress Pridgett's left eye. Then suddenly, she pursed her lips and blew gently on the eye. Mistress Pridgett blinked and rubbed her eye. The woman had vanished from in front of her. She could see everything else, but only with her right eye, and she could see no fairies with it, for that was not the eye that had been touched by the ointment.

So that was the end of it for Mistress Pridgett, as far as her second sight was concerned. She never did regain the vision in her left eye. But she still had the use of her right eye, for which she was thankful, since it served her for all she needed. And she still had the use of the gold coins the fairy man had given her, for which she was also thankful, since that was quite enough to comfort her for the rest of the long, happy and uneventful life she had yet to lead.

WHAT DO YOU THINK?
QUESTIONS TO PONDER

Do you think that the way we normally see the world is the way it really is?

Might it be possible to have a 'second sight'? What might the world look like from this perspective?

Is it possible to see the world simultaneously through different worldviews, in the way Mistress Pridgett did through her different eyes?

PHILOSOPHICAL CONUNDRUMS:
DO WE SEE THE WORLD AS IT TRULY IS?

From the very origins of philosophy in Greek thought, there has been a persistent worry amongst philosophers that there may be a 'real' world which is different from the world we think we live in. The thinking here is that, in forming our views of the world, all we have to rely upon are our senses. But how do we know our senses can be relied upon? Perhaps an evil demon is tricking us into thinking the world is as it appears to us. Perhaps an evil scientist is keeping our brains in vats and is tricking these brains into thinking we are leading our normal, everyday lives.

Such scenarios may seem unlikely … but it is not the *likelihood* of one of these scenarios being true that is at issue here, but rather its mere *possibility*. For if it is possible, then we must also face the possibility that anything – perhaps, *everything* – we think we 'know' about the 'world' may be wrong. We must face the possibility that we can *never* know anything with certainty. These thought experiments challenge the most basic, common-sense beliefs we have about our world. They lead us to doubt what we think we know. They lead, in other words, to a philosophical theory we call 'scepticism'.

What is it about the story of Mistress Pridgett that leads in the same direction? The story grants that there is a way that humans normally see the world under normal circumstances. Yet the normality of this way of seeing the world is no guarantee of its truth. Others see it differently. The fact that there are other ways of seeing the world – no matter their cause – is sufficient to challenge our ordinary beliefs about the way the world is. Mistress Pridgett's 'second sight' is thus a metaphor for another, different view of the world. While she has her second sight, Mistress Pridgett sees two contrasting worldviews and switches between them. When she loses it, her view of the world is diminished. It is no longer as comprehensive as it was. Is our 'normal' view of reality limited in this same way?

The study of scepticism takes us into a fascinating field of philosophy called epistemology, the study of knowledge. Epistemology asks: what is knowledge? What can we know with certainty? How do we know what we know? How are knowledge claims justified? In this field, scepticism is the theory that our beliefs about reality lack the justification we normally claim for them.

There are various forms of scepticism, which pose different degrees of challenge to our beliefs. The mildest form lies in the simple admission that we could always be wrong. We find this form of scepticism in Plato's account of the philosophy of his mentor, Socrates, whose ideas Plato developed in the years following Socrates' death in 399 BC. In Plato's writings, Socrates is reported to have said he does not know anything. Later philosophers presented this claim paradoxically: 'All I know is that I know nothing'.

Paradoxes such as this, as we shall see later in this volume, are normally thought to pose a serious problem for philosophy. Not so for Socrates. Convinced of his own ignorance, Socrates made it the basis of a method for doing philosophy. The 'Socratic method' is a style of repeated questioning, starting with the question-form 'what is …?' and proceeding to challenge a believer's most basic beliefs about the topic under discussion.

Such questioning shows when our beliefs are unsubstantiated or unjustified. This method remains a model for the acquisition of knowledge, by constantly testing its limits.

A much stronger form of scepticism, by contrast, was reportedly held by Socrates' rival, Protagoras. This form of scepticism is more destructive in its effects. Claiming that 'man is the measure of all things', Protagoras held that our beliefs are inevitably the product of our own personal experiences, which are inevitably limited. For each of us, then, the world is as it appears to be.

In this strong form, scepticism is related to a stance known as relativism. Like scepticism, relativism comes in different forms, but comes down to the idea that we have no criteria for deciding what is ultimately or objectively true. There can be no absolute truth about reality because any claim to truth will be relative to the person making that claim. The variability of human perception undermines its status as evidence for our beliefs about reality. That is to say, the fact that we all see the world differently means we have no objective evidence for any claims about the way the world 'really' is.

Some sceptics, such as the 2nd century Roman philosopher Sextus Empiricus, argued that a robust scepticism such as this brings peace of mind, because it counters our frustration at being constantly thwarted in our quest for truth. Sextus recommended suspending belief, living in accordance with our natural inclinations or with local customs. A philosopher is likely to respond: why even bother getting up in the morning? When Socrates commented that 'the unexamined life is not worth living', he meant that, if we do no more than follow our desires – or other people – we live at the level of beasts.

How do we overcome the strongest and most destructive forms of scepticism? Is it possible to know *anything*? The simplest way to overcome relativism is to note that it is obviously self-refuting. The theory of relativism is itself a claim to knowledge. If *all* claims are relative to a given perspective and therefore limited, then the relativist's claims are also limited in this same way. The theory suffers from its all-encompassing scope: it undermines *everything*, including itself. It is simply implausible to say that relativism is true for Protagoras, on the basis of his experience of the world, but false for those of us to don't accept it, on the basis of ours.

So much for relativism, you might say. But there does appear to be some truth in the idea that our perspective on the world will be a product of our situation within it – at least to some degree. The standard example here is the Inuit, who have many different names for the different types of snow they encounter in their lives, while for the rest of us, one or two names suffice. This example may not actually involve a difference of worldviews: perhaps the Inuit is merely making finer distinctions within a worldview that is shared with others, just as an artist may see finer gradations of colour than is common. But the point about the diversity of human perspectives may still hold true.

Here, it is helpful to distinguish between two different types of perspective we may have: our views about what *is* the case and our views about what *should be* the case. The 'situated' nature of worldviews is especially evident in our *values*: our views about what *should* be the case. This becomes apparent when we compare the world's different religious and ethical systems, which disagree on even the most basic of issues. Is the same true of *facts*: our views about what *is* the case? One response to scepticism has been to insist on this distinction between values and facts. Many philosophers have been happy to admit the relativity of values, if only to defend, by contrast, the objectivity of facts.

So, for example, as the modern sciences were establishing themselves in the 18th century, a Scottish philosopher by the name of David Hume declared that, if we take any scholarly book, we can ask two questions. Does it contain questions of '*abstract* reasoning' that can be tested by the laws of logic? Does it contain questions of '*experimental* reasoning' about 'matters of fact and existence' that can be tested by the sciences? If it contains neither, then we should 'commit it to the flames' for it contains nothing but 'illusion'.

Hume's is an important expression of a form of scepticism that has been influential throughout modern philosophy. With these words, Hume assesses human knowledge using a criterion of 'verifiability' – that is, our ability to *prove* whether a statement is either true or false. Statements of 'reason' and statements of 'fact or existence' can both be proven, either by logic or by experience.

But nothing outside these fields deserves the title of knowledge, according to Hume, because it is in principle *unverifiable*: it cannot be proven to be true or false. I leave it to the reader to decide how much of this volume is left to us, once Hume's inferno has been fed. Most of this book falls outside Hume's two neat categories … but then, Hume's own writings do just the same!

CHAPTER THREE

THE DREAMER

Frederico was a sunny young man with a mop of red hair and an easy smile. He lived with his father and they would have been as happy as the day is long, but for one thing: they were poor. They were as poor as the little mice chased by the cat around their tumbledown house. Their house, truth to tell, resembled a hut more than anything, but it was well-located, for it sat neatly on its own patch of lawn, with a wide and pleasant river at the front of it and an old and beautiful apple tree at the back. They had a hard life, but they neither grumbled nor complained, since who was there to listen but the cat?

One night, while Frederico was sleeping soundly, he had a dream. In this dream, a tall and stately gentleman dressed in flowing robes came to him. He said, 'Frederico, I know you have had a hard life and have neither grumbled nor complained. I would like to help you. Listen carefully: follow the path along the river until you find a bridge. On the other side of the river, you will see a town. Stand on the bridge and wait there. It may be that nothing will happen on the first day and it may be that nothing will happen on the second day either, but wait patiently and, perhaps on the third day, someone will come to you and tell you something that will be good for you.'

In the morning, Frederico remembered his dream and told it to his father. 'I have half a mind to follow the man's advice,' he said. 'It would be a curious thing if what he said were true.'

'Nonsense,' replied his father. 'It was only a dream and a dream cannot be true. You'd much better spend your day going to Mrs Godwin's and earning some pennies chopping her wood.' Frederico did as his father asked and worked all day chopping Mrs Godwin's wood and by the evening, he had earned a few pennies and forgotten all about his dream.

That night, however, the gentleman in the flowing robes visited Frederico's dreams a second time: 'Why have you not done as I told you, Frederico? Good fortune does not wait on any man. You must set out tomorrow and go to the bridge and be there when your fortune arrives.'

When Frederico woke the next morning, his first thought was to set out and find the bridge of which the man spoke. 'I am truly of a mind to follow the man's advice,' he told his father. 'Fortune waits on no man and I must be there if it should come.'

'Don't be foolish, Frederico,' replied his father. 'Dreams are only dreams. They don't tell us anything about the real world. If they did, they would tell you that Mr Stanley's hedges need trimming.' So Frederico did not set out in search of his fortune that day either.

That night, the gentleman in flowing robes came to Frederico a third time. This time, he came in the morning, just before Frederico awoke, when his dreams were the most vivid and compelling. The man's face was stern and his look was forbidding: 'Fool! Three times now I have come to you and now I will come no more. Go to the bridge near the town and listen out for what you may hear. Otherwise want and hardship will follow you all the days of your life.' With this warning, the man disappeared and Frederico awoke.

This time, it was no use for his father to argue with him. As the man had commanded, so Frederico intended to do. He stopped only long enough to put some food in his mouth and some more in his pockets and he set off, one foot in front of the other.

For some hours, Frederico journeyed down the river, until he was footsore and weary. He was starting to wonder how long he would have to continue travelling, when finally he saw a bridge that crossed the river and on the other side of it was a town. Frederico was uncertain, but he felt that this must be the place the gentleman had spoken about.

Frederico found a convenient place to stand on the bridge and there he stood. The passers-by stared at him, wondering what he was doing standing by so idly. Some of them said good day and some of them spoke to him of this and that, but not a soul said anything that might, by any chance, be conceived as good fortune.

All that day, Frederico waited on the bridge and all the day after as well. By the third day, Frederico had eaten every morsel in his pockets and was fast exhausting the interest of the townspeople, who started to ignore him. Then, naturally, he began to wonder whether he was entirely foolish to be loitering on the bridge day after day, all because of a dream, when he might be earning pennies at home, one way or another.

Now, on the other side of the bridge, there was a tailor's shop, where a tailor sat and looked out over the bridge as he stitched. The tailor was an inquisitive man. Ever since Frederico had taken up his place on the bridge, the tailor had been staring out his window and wondering why Frederico was standing there and what his business might be. The longer Frederico stood there, the more curious the tailor became. He watched and wondered, and fidgeted and fussed, until he could no longer work at his stitching for all his curiosity. Putting aside his work, he walked out of his shop and onto the bridge, to ask Frederico what he was doing there.

'Good day,' the tailor greeted Frederico. 'I wonder, are you waiting here for someone?'

'I am and I am not,' Frederico replied.

'What do you mean by that?' asked the tailor. 'How can you be waiting and not waiting, all at once?'

'I am waiting for someone, that is true,' Frederico explained, 'but I do not know who it is I am waiting for, nor when he or she will come, nor, for that matter, whether he or she will come at all.' And Frederico told the tailor about his dream and how he had had been told to wait on the bridge for someone to come and tell him something that would make his fortune.

'What a silly fellow you are!' laughed the tailor. 'I too have dreamed dreams, but I have far too much sense to pay any attention to them. Why, only last week I dreamed about a gentleman dressed in flowing robes who told me to walk over the bridge and along the river until I came to a tumbledown hut. There, he said, at the back of the hut, I should dig among the roots of an old apple tree. There, he said, I would find a chest filled with money.'

'That is what I dreamed. But did I go wandering off in search of such a place? Not in the least! I stuck to my work and I earned my pennies and haven't given it another moment's thought until now. A hut with an apple tree and a chest filled with money? How good it might have been if it weren't just a dream.'

So the man said goodbye and went back over the bridge to the tailor's shop. He settled himself back down again and picked up his work and started stitching.

Frederico stood there on the bridge, scratching his head. He thought for a while about what the tailor had said … and then he turned on his heels and set off for home. The further we went, the more of a hurry he was in until at last, when he was within sight of his house, he was all out of breath with the haste he was in.

He did not go inside, but shouted to his father to come out, while he raced to fetch a pick and shovel. Taking up the pick, he began digging around the roots of the apple tree. He had not dug for long when his pick struck something hard. Flinging the pick aside and seizing the shovel, he set to work and soon uncovered a chest made of stout oak and bound around with metal bands. The chest was so heavy, he and his father could hardly lift it from the hole he had made in the roots of the tree.

The chest was fastened with a great metal lock, but that mattered little. Frederico took to the lock with his pick and, with a few swift blows, it was lying in pieces on the grass. He lifted the lid and then fell to his knees beside the chest. There were enough gold and silver coins to keep Frederico and his father in comfort for the rest of their days. They hauled the chest into the hut and spent the rest of the evening counting the coins, one by one.

Frederico built a fine house where the hut had been, between the river and the old apple tree. He started to dress in very fine clothes, to eat very fine food and to keep very fine company. Sometimes, he would hire a coach to take him into the town, where he would dine with friends or attend the theatre. His father preferred to stay at home, curled up in front of the fire with a good book and the cat sleeping contentedly on his lap.

And so you see, that was the way fortune came to Frederico … and it was all because of a dream.

One day, Frederico put on a fine suit and walked along the path by the river, over the bridge to the town and into to the tailor's shop. He found the tailor sitting there, looking out over the bridge as he stitched.

'Good day,' Frederico addressed him. 'Do you remember me?'

'No, your lordship,' answered the tailor, bowing low, 'I have not had the honour.' Evidently he thought of Frederico as someone of great importance.

Frederico did not have the heart to tell the tailor that he was the ragged fellow who had stood waiting on the bridge, nor that, if the tailor had only followed the advice of his dream, he too might now be mistaken for a lord. There is no reason to tell people they are wrong if they do not wish to follow their dreams. But he did place an order with the tailor for a wardrobe of very fine suits and was sure to pay for them very handsomely indeed.

What do you think?
Questions to Ponder

Was Frederico wrong to follow the gentleman's advice, rather than the advice of his father?

Can a dream inform you of something you did not previously know? Is it possible to discover something in a dream?

Are you actually 'yourself' in a dream? For example, could a good person think or act in a way that is morally evil in a dream?

PHILOSOPHICAL CONUNDRUMS:
CAN A DREAM BE TRUE?

In his *Meditations on First Philosophy*, the 17th century French philosopher René Descartes describes sitting beside his fire, his papers in hand and candle on the table beside him, being as sure of the truth of his perceptions as anyone has a right to be. But then an unsettling thought occurs to him: how do I know that my perceptions of this fire, these papers, this candle, represent the truth about reality? When I am asleep and dreaming, I also think that my perceptions represent the truth – but they do not. I am deceived by my dreams into thinking I am sitting by the fire, when in fact I am asleep in bed. Might I now be in bed dreaming? How do I know I am not?

Modern philosophy is sometimes said to have started with this image of Descartes, sitting in his armchair by the fire, asking, 'How do I know that I am not now dreaming?' It started, that is, with a question about dreams. Descartes' question is whether we might be systematically misled by our dreams into believing things that are untrue. This is the problem of 'dream scepticism'.

Descartes' question is clearly sceptical, like those we discussed in the last chapter, but is also a question of the special nature of dreams and their relation to reality. In this, it is related to the question posed by Frederico in the story above. Frederico asks: is it possible for a dream to tell us something that is true? Could we discover the truth in a dream? Like Descartes, he is asking whether dreams are inevitably a source of deception. Let's start with Descartes' question, since it has been much discussed, to see whether an answer emerges to Frederico's question as well.

Descartes' dream scepticism proceeds from the claim, which he takes to be evident, that dreams are deceptive. To this, he adds a second claim: we have no sure criterion for knowing whether we are awake or whether we are asleep and dreaming. Let's give this idea a name, so that we can talk about it: let's call it the

'Indistinguishability Problem'. The Indistinguishability Problem is the problem of distinguishing between waking and dream life.

A first line of defence against dream scepticism, then, might be to challenge the idea that dream and waking life are indistinguishable, to show that there are clear differences between them. We might note, for example, that our waking experiences have a greater *coherence* than our dream experiences and connect more seamlessly to the larger course of our lives. So the fact that our waking life is not normally absurd – in the way are dreams often are – is a sure sign of its difference from dream life.

Such an approach does not solve the Indistinguishability Problem, however. While our dreams are sometimes absurd, they are not always so. Some people report having lucid dreams, in which they become aware that they are dreaming. This may help distinguish waking and dream experiences on occasion, but it does not help with non-lucid dreams, which most of us have most of the time. The fact that our dreams are *sometimes* indistinguishable from waking experiences is sufficient to generate doubt about our waking experiences. The similarity between waking and dreaming experiences need not be total, but merely sufficient to introduce doubt.

It seems we need to double down, then, and challenge the claim that dreams and waking experiences *ever* have the same content. As far back as the 5th century, the theologian Augustine lamented that his dream experiences belonged to a 'dream self' which bore little resemblance to his 'true self'. This led him to draw a distinction between 'actions', which occur in our waking life, and 'happenings', which occur in our dream life. Augustine was not *acting* in his dream life, he claimed, but undergoing an experience which was *happening* to him, over which he had no control. In this way, he absolved himself of responsibility for whatever misdeeds his ill-behaved dream self might perform.

Following Augustine, we might say that, in dreams, we do not actually *believe* something to be the case; rather we *imagine* it to be so. Imaginings are neither true nor false. If dreams do not involve beliefs, they too are neither truthful nor deceptive. Our beliefs – that is, our beliefs of waking life – are untouched by any of our imaginings, waking or dreaming. Thinking about our story, then, we might say that Frederico is motivated, not by the belief that the knowing gentleman of his dreams is telling the truth, but by his imagining that it might be so.

Does this solve the problem of distinguishing dream and waking experiences? Sadly, it seems not. For if an 'imagining' is *experienced* in a way that is indistinguishable from a 'belief', then doubt returns. For the problem that led Descartes to doubt his perceptions was a subjective one. Descartes did not claim that dream and waking experiences were in no way different *in themselves*. Rather the problem was that they were indistinguishable *subjectively*, on the level of experience. Indeed, it's the very fact that they *are* different – one is generally truthful and the other generally deceptive – that makes their subjective indistinguishability a problem.

What did Descartes propose, then? Descartes' response to dream scepticism was to locate a single feature of his waking experience which, he held, was undeniable. This would be the criterion for distinguishing waking and dreaming experiences. The single feature he identified was the thinking of his waking self. While he was thinking – 'Am I not now dreaming?' – one thing certainly existed: this thought. And, since he was sure of the existence of his thinking, he could also be sure of his own existence as a 'thinking substance'. Hence, his famous dictum: 'I think, therefore I am'.

There has been a great deal of debate within philosophy about whether this dictum actually responds to the Indistinguishability Problem, as Descartes himself set it up, in the way he hoped. Could his dream self not also believe itself to be thinking? Could the experience of 'thinking' of the dream self and experience of thinking of the waking self not also be indistinguishable?

If we are to overcome dream scepticism, it seems that we need to challenge the claim that waking and dreaming are *experienced* in the same way. We need to be able to distinguish between our *experiences* of waking and dreaming. This seems at first difficult: when we are in the midst of a dream, we naturally think we are awake and experiencing as normal. So we tend to think of dreams as like other experiences, occurring in real time and under the same subjective conditions we normally experience in wakefulness.

On closer inspection, however, the experience of a dream is not actually like that. All we know of our dreams is a recollection after the fact: a dream report. This recollection is concrete evidence that a dream has occurred, but it provides no evidence that it occurred in the way our waking experiences occur. The dream may, for all we know, have occurred in a single moment. It may, for all we know, have been implanted in our minds in the seconds before we woke. Importantly, the dream report is not the experience itself, but merely an impression we have, after the event, of a dream having occurred. And this suggests that a dream is a different type of experience from a waking experience – if indeed it is an 'experience' at all.

Whether this analysis overcomes the problem of distinguishing waking and dreaming experiences deserves further attention. If this analysis is correct, however, it does at least give us an answer to Frederico's question: can dreams be true? On standard definitions of 'truth', we expect a true belief to be justified – or at least justifiable – on the basis of evidence. Our analysis suggests that dream experiences are not sufficiently reliable as to be evidence for the truth of a belief. Frederico's father is correct, it seems: a dream belief cannot be true, except perhaps by accident.

There is anecdotal evidence – that is, evidence people obtain from their experiences – to suggest that sometimes dreams tell people things they 'know' subconsciously, but have not yet brought into consciousness. This may be an explanation for reports that people 'discover' things in their dreams: the inventions the dreamer had been working on, the problems they were unable to solve, are processed subconsciously, brought to consciousness in a dream and then recollected afterwards in the usual way.

This may not explain the certainty of Frederico's belief in the truth of the gentleman's prediction. Nor does it fully account for the anecdotal evidence of dreamers who claim that they 'just knew' something – something they could not have previously known – as a result of a dream. Might this be because dreams unleash the powers of the imagination, which operate according to laws that are different from the mundane laws of cause and effect we expect of wakeful experience?

Chapter Four

The Invisible Gardener

A long time ago, in a cabin on the shores of a great ocean, there lived a wise man by the name of Thomas. He lived by himself, devoting himself to his studies. He sought from the stars and the sea, and from the animals and plants, the truths of nature which only great minds understand. He was a gentle soul, much loved by those who knew him, and so he occasionally received visitors, with whom he enjoyed sharing his discoveries on the wonders of nature.

One day, Thomas received a visitor, in the form of a dear old friend who came with wonderful tale to tell. Thomas' visitor told how he had been travelling along the coast in his small boat to visit Thomas when he had been thrown off course by turbulent seas. After some time, seeing a golden coastline in the distance, he sought haven in a secluded bay. He had landed on an island of such rare beauty that words failed him at this point in his story.

'Such an island it was!' the visitor enthused. 'Truly, a paradise such as even you cannot imagine! I could not possibly describe it to you, my friend, were I to try for all eternity. The gods and goddesses alone know such beauty!' As the sun set over the ocean and the day passed into a warm and tranquil evening, the visitor settled into a quiet reverie of the marvels of the island he had recently quitted. A blissful smile crept across his face, attracting the glow of the moonlight.

Naturally, Thomas found himself intrigued by his visitor's tale and wanting to know more about the island. His visitor could tell him no more. 'Come! You must see it for yourself,' is all he could say. 'Come with me, we will explore this island together. Nothing would make me happier than to share it with you.' In time, Thomas allowed himself to be persuaded to leave the peace and calm of his home, and to share the adventure of the search for the island. So he too was on board when his friend eventually set sail again.

The passage to the island was a long one. Thomas had to exercise all he knew of the movements of the stars to chart its course. On the way, they saw wonderful things: the playfulness of the dolphins that hurled themselves out of the water alongside their boat; the majesty of great flocks of birds that winged extraordinary distances from their winter to their summer homes. But nothing prepared Thomas for the wonders he beheld when he finally stepped onto the shores of the magnificent island. Surveying the vista, he had the impression that all the world's splendours had been distilled into a single sunlit diorama.

Over the days and weeks that followed, Thomas and his friend set themselves the task of exploring the island. They found streams of crystal clarity from which to drink and orchards of delicious fruit to eat. They found a phantasmagoria of animals and plants, causing Thomas to giggle with excitement. But the best was yet to come. For, one day, while rambling through unfamiliar terrain, the two friends stumbled upon a hidden gem: a garden of such surpassing beauty that its existence appeared as some sort of miracle to the travellers.

The garden was not large, but it was perfectly proportioned. Around the garden was a fringe of tall trees, creating the effect of an enclosed dell. The dell was a tumult of colour: plants of every texture and hue could be seen from every vantage and their cool scent wafted on a gentle breeze. Thomas imagined that, if magical folk had ever existed, this must be the place from which they had originally come.

Thomas' friend was dumbstruck. He stood staring in awe and wonder. When finally he found his tongue, he spoke in a whisper, as if he could not bear to disturb a single leaf of the garden: 'Look at the colours of those petals! Look at the shape of those blooms! How can such a garden exist? What gardener is responsible for it?' he pondered. 'I don't believe that a garden such as this can have come to be on its own. It is not possible. Some god or goddess must have planted it and must be tending it even still. How else could such perfection exist?'

Thomas was doubtful. He admitted that the garden was more perfect than anything else they had seen on their travels, but he did not believe that it was of an entirely different nature from these other things. The vaulting dolphins, the winging birds: these he knew to be wonders of nature, which it had been his life's work to study. The beauty of the garden might have been different in degree, but it was not different in kind, from other natural things.

'The garden is certainly enchanting, but I see no evidence of anyone tending it,' he admitted to his friend. 'No gods or goddesses reside here, as far as I can see. The growth I see here is not the work of a gardener. It is entirely natural. The garden came to be by its own devices. It grows like this as a result of the laws of its own nature.'

Thomas and his friend debated the origins of the beautiful garden at great length. Thomas saw nothing to lead him to a belief that a divine gardener tended the garden, while his friend was aghast that Thomas refused to see the evidence right in front of his eyes: the garden itself, in all its perfection. Surprised and challenged by the depth of their disagreement, the two friends chose to stay on the island until they could resolve the question of how the garden had come to be.

They visited the garden often. Thomas' friend tried to demonstrate to him the clear evidence for the gardener, but the gardener remained steadfastly invisible to Thomas. Thomas explained to his friend the laws of science, as he understood them, that caused the garden to develop as it did. His friend understood these laws, but insisted that it made no difference to his view that the garden was ultimately the work of a divine gardener. It was as if the two friends were looking at the garden through differently coloured spectacles – or simply through different eyes.

The friends talked and argued; they analysed the issue from this angle and that. At times, they grew exasperated with each other, though never so much as to undermine their friendship. In time, however – there being seemingly no way to resolve the difference of opinion between them – they slowly put the question of the existence of an invisible gardener to rest. They continued to delight in their strolls through the island, but spoke of other things. Soon enough, they felt it was time to return to their everyday lives.

So Thomas left the island unconvinced in the existence of the god or the goddess to whom his friend credited the island's enchantment. The friends retraced their travels and Thomas was dropped at his home, returning to peace and calm and to his studies of the stars and seas, the animals and plants. He learnt a great deal about the world around him and became extremely knowledgeable.

The years passed. Thomas's hair took on a distinguished shade of silver and his eyes started to weaken, though his mind remained quick and sure. His friend visited him on occasion and they spoke of the island fondly, as the happiest of their shared memories, but never revisited the question of the invisible gardener that had so perplexed them during their stay there.

And then one day, Thomas received a letter which made tears swell in his eyes and spill over the tall, elegant script on the page. 'By the time you receive this letter, my dearest friend, I shall be gone,' his friend wrote. 'Please do not mourn for me. I am content. I have led a happy life and the happiest of my memories are the days we spent together on the enchanted island. It was there that I learned the infinite goodness of the being who tends this earth. Blessed am I, that I may find peace in the hands of the god or goddess who created such beauty and shared it with us so generously!'

Thomas did not abide by the sender's request: he mourned his friend very deeply. But that was not the only effect of the letter. As the days and weeks passed, Thomas found that the letter had reminded him of his visit to the island. This visit was now playing on his mind: had his friend been right to say that the island was tended by a god or a goddess? Had he missed something important in dismissing his friend's claims? Had a god or a goddess tried to show him something miraculous, which he had simply failed to see?

So Thomas began collecting the wood, sailcloth and other materials needed to build a boat that would carry him once again over the seas. He went out with local fishermen to obtain the skills he needed to steer his boat through the most turbulent weather. He set himself diligently to studying the stars, recalling the route he took on his original journey with his friend. Slowly, piece by piece, he built his boat. As the boat grew, so did Thomas' determination to rediscover the enchanted island.

How to describe Thomas' excitement when, one spring day, he set out across tranquil seas in the direction he had charted? As night fell, the stars appeared as a path which led him onwards. It was as if the entire Milky Way were constructed precisely to direct him towards his most cherished goal: to walk once more in the gardens of the island.

Thomas sailed his boat over shifting seas for many days and nights. On some days, the weather reflected his peace of mind, when he saw again the dolphins jumping to greet him and the birds tipping their wings as they winged toward their summer homes. On other days, the weather reflected his fears: was he even capable of locating the island and, if he did, would it give him the answers he was looking for?

For all his fears, there came a day when the white sand shone below a glorious summer sun and Thomas stepped onto the shores of the island once again. Little had changed over the years. He found again the garden where he had strolled with his friend and where they had enjoyed the pleasure of discussing the power that had created the rich and splendid fabric of life spread out before them.

The journey had nevertheless exhausted Thomas. He knew he no longer had the energy to complete the trip homewards all by himself, were he even sure of the path he should steer. So he contented himself with making a small clearing in the garden he had discovered so long ago and there he made his home. Using his knowledge of plants and animals, he tended the living things that provided him with food and clothing. He befriended the animals who lived there and, in his gentleness, received a grudging respect from the animals that might naturally have sought to kill a visitor such as he. If he felt lonely, he spoke to these animals and to his friend. He even believed he heard his friend laughing on occasion, when Thomas shared a joke he knew would amuse him.

Thomas never did see evidence of a visit of the god or goddess in whom his friend believed … well, not exactly. He worked so long in the garden that, at a certain point, it would have been difficult to say who had contributed precisely what to its prosperity. He knew well that his friend would have seen the contentment of Thomas' life on the island as further evidence for what he had been saying all along. Over time, however, Thomas became quite comfortable in admitting to himself that he simply was not sure who was right. Perhaps later, if at last he joined his friend in another, higher world, he would finally know the truth.

What do you think?
Questions to ponder

Who do you agree with: Thomas or his friend? Was the garden's perfection evidence for the existence of a god or goddess?

Must we always have evidence for our beliefs? Is it right to hold some beliefs on the basis of faith, rather than on the basis of reason? Which ones?

Could the existence of God be decided on the basis of reason, do you think? Should it be?

Philosophical conundrums:
Does God exist?

If, on having established the truth of his existence to his own satisfaction, Descartes had held fast to the scepticism that led him to doubt it in the first place, then his journey from doubt to certainty about the existence of the world around him would have been very slow going indeed. How, he admitted, can you ever find truths that are as certain as that of your own existence?

Fortunately – or so Descartes believed – he happened to have on his side a good and gracious God, whom he knew would not deceive him in systematic ways. It was by leveraging his certainty in the existence of God that Descartes came in turn to establish the existence of the world around him. But of course he had a problem: although he believed in the truth of God's existence on grounds of faith, how could he prove it on grounds of reason? Is there any *evidence* for God's existence? Is there *reason* for belief?

We owe the outline of the story of the invisible gardener to a debate which occurred in the middle of the last century between two great figures of English philosophy: Antony Flew and John Wisdom. The story itself was proposed by Wisdom, who conceived it as a 'parable' similar to the those of the New Testament, such as the Parables of the Sower and the Good Samaritan. A parable is a story that is held to reveal a deeper truth. I have developed Wisdom's parable significantly and given it characters, to reflect not merely the philosophy, but also the psychology, of religious belief. Thomas' name is a reference to 'doubting Thomas', the biblical figure who doubted the evidence of Jesus' resurrection when it stood directly in front of him.

The debate between Flew and Wisdom occurred in the context of a broader argument over the need of the believer to have solid evidence for their beliefs. A philosopher by the name of William Clifford had earlier argued that it is wrong – *always* and *everywhere* – to believe *anything* on insufficient evidence. This dramatic claim helped support the belief that metaphysical claims – claims about the existence of God, for example – are inherently misguided because there is simply no evidence for them, one way or the other.

It is not difficult to fabricate examples to show that Clifford's criterion for evidence is overly burdensome and that we quite reasonably assume our beliefs to be true, even without solid evidence, in order simply to function in the world. We naturally take the advice of strangers whom we stop for directions on the street, for example, with no further justification than a simple trust that people are generally well-meaning and honest.

In his Parable of the Invisible Gardener, however, Wisdom asks a deeper question about what qualifies as evidence itself. He argues that religious believers do indeed have evidence for their belief in God's existence: this evidence might be found, among other places, in the beauty of this world. Wisdom is building on earlier arguments, going back hundreds of years, that the *design* of the universe is evidence that it must have been *designed* – by a Grand Designer, no less, whom we call 'God'. This argument is justly famous: it is called the Ontological Argument for the Existence of God. Descartes himself relied heavily on this argument in his proof of God's existence. The Ontological Argument remains a topic of intense debate in philosophical circles.

To justify the claims of the religious believer, Wisdom suggests that the argument between the believer (the theist) and the non-believer (the atheist) is not that they disagree about what the evidence tells them. Rather, they disagree about what *counts* as evidence in the first place. Wisdom argues that it is perfectly reasonable for a religious believer to believe in God on the basis of the evidence they see around them. Flew responds that 'the evidence they see around them' is no evidence at all.

Think of this debate by analogy with evidence for the existence of less contentious things. We quite reasonably take a broken window and missing possessions in our house as evidence for the existence of a burglar in our neighbourhood. We do not need to see the burglar in person to know that he or she exists, nor to justify our belief that he or she has visited our house. So too, says the theist, the evidence of God's handiwork justifies belief in God.

One argument against this analogy is that, although we may not actually have seen the burglar, there is no reason why we *couldn't* have seen him or her, had we been home at the time of their visit. Had we installed a monitoring system, we could have recorded the visit. So, in principle, there is no difficulty obtaining direct evidence of the burglar, beyond the indirect evidence: the broken window and missing possessions.

That is not the end of it, however. The religious believer may respond that, while the *indirect* evidence of God is like that of the burglar, God and the burglar are entirely different in themselves and so we cannot expect *direct* evidence of their existence to take the same form. God is not a material being like a burglar, so it is wrong to expect God to appear in the same way a burglar does. Indeed, it is to decide the outcome of the argument in advance to decree that evidence must be material in form, like the evidence of a monitoring system. We cannot rule out in advance the possibility of evidence in other forms.

American philosopher John Hick has noted more recently that, if life continues after death in some manner, then this too would provide evidence to justify religious belief. This is not evidence the living are likely to obtain, admittedly, but it is in principle evidence nonetheless – as Thomas himself acknowledged as he lived out his last days in the enchanted garden. What might the atheist reply to that?

The debate over the Parable of the Invisible Gardener is a good example of the back-and-forth nature of philosophical argument. It is also a good example of how debate in one field of philosophy – over the existence of God in the philosophy of religion – influences and is influenced by debate in other fields of philosophy – over the nature of evidence in epistemology, the philosophy of knowledge.

In this story, our protagonist Thomas appears to resolve the question of God's existence to his own satisfaction on epistemological grounds. Sidestepping the arguments of both theist and atheist, Thomas adopts the standpoint of the agnostic who, having carefully weighed the arguments this way and that, is content to declare: 'I simply do not know.'

CHAPTER FIVE

THE GREAT MR HARMAN

Mr Zachary Burton gazed out his dining room window onto the garden. His sister Zoe, who was visiting with her daughter Amelie, saw that he was in a meditative mood. So, swallowing the last mouthful of her lunch, she put down her knife and fork and turned to her brother: 'Zach, I was thinking of Mr Harman last night. Do you remember Mr Harman?'

Zachary, a middle-aged man of slightly impish appearance, pretended to be shocked: 'Harman? *Of course* I remember Harman. Of all the faces from my childhood, there is none I remember so well! He had a low forehead ...'

'Straw hair,' Zoe added.

'Squinty eyes,' Zachary continued.

'His cheekbones were high and pointed and red.'

'He was thin, bent, somewhat feeble in appearance ...'

'...but actually strong and dextrous!' Zoe finished.

Zachary hesitated. 'We forgot the ears.'

'Oh! We'll have to start all over again!' Zoe laughed.

The siblings gave their recital of Harman's features in a monotonous tone, but with barely suppressed merriment. Amelie listened to the strange performance somewhat doubtfully. The two eventually stopped and turned to her. 'From our earliest childhood,' Zachary explained, 'Harman was an article of faith in our household.'

'I don't understand,' said Amelie.

'That's because we've never told you about Harman. At one time, he was the most notorious member of this entire community. Your grandfather held him in the highest esteem and often spoke of him.'

'So who was he, then?' ventured Amelie … and her mother and uncle replied with a simultaneous guffaw. Amelie found it odd that the two of them, so different from each other, should nevertheless find the same thing quite so hilariously funny as they evidently did.

Finally, Amelie's mother took pity on her: 'Harman started out as a gardener, who came to fix up this garden here. But then he moved on to other occupations, not quite so wholesome.' Her eyes twinkled.

'Do you remember, Zach, when Papa could not find his pen or scissors or gloves, he would say, "I do believe Mr Harman has been here!"'

'Harman's reputation was not good,' Zachary agreed. 'A sad thing!' he spluttered.

'Is that all?' asked Amelie.

'No, my sweet, that is not all, not by a long way,' her mother replied.

'No,' Zachary agreed. 'For Harman was most notorious in this … that, while he was more familiar to us than anyone else alive, nevertheless …'

'… he didn't even *exist*!' Zoe chimed in, triumphantly.

'How could you say such a thing, Zoe?' demanded Zachary, in mock outrage. 'Of course Harman existed! It is true that it was a rather peculiar sort of existence … Let us just say that Harman was not born like others. He was born fully-grown.'

'I understand less and less,' said Amelie, starting to tire of the adults' riddles.

Zachary settled himself deep into his chair, finally embarking on the explanation: 'When my parents married, they moved into this house in the hope of a quiet, peaceful country life. They thought they'd found it until a distant relative of my mother's appeared one day on the doorstep. Aunt Pauline – that's what we called her

– lived in a large house not far from here and she decided that, since they were relatives, my father and mother must dine with her on Sundays. There was apparently no escape from this ancient familial custom. It was the *proper* thing to do.'

'Now Aunt Pauline was a demanding woman. These Sunday visits continued for some time and became increasingly dreadful, until my father was bored to the point of tears. When my parents refused an invitation, Aunt Pauline would send a servant to pick them up, for those were the days when servants did the dirty work for the wealthy. My father finally rebelled and swore to accept no more of Aunt Pauline's invitations, telling my mother to find some suitable excuse. Unfortunately, my mother was not good at pretence.'

'Not true, not true! She could fib as well as anyone when she chose,' Zoe corrected him. 'When my father developed whooping cough, she said, "Thank goodness, now we'll be free of Aunt Pauline for weeks!" But then my father improved, unfortunately, and Aunt Pauline arrived at the door to say they were expected the following Sunday. So my mother did what any devoted wife would do. She lied through her teeth: "I am extremely sorry, dear Aunt, but that will be impossible. On Sunday, we are expecting the gardener."'

Amelie, Zoe and Zachary involuntarily turned their heads to the small square of garden out the window. A gardener had clearly never once set foot among the withering plants.

'It was no different in your grandparents' day,' Zachary admitted sheepishly, taking over the explanation again. 'Well, Aunt Pauline looked out at the garden and exclaimed, "You're expecting a *gardener*? *Whatever for*?" Mother suddenly realised the improbability of her excuse.'

'Aunt Pauline became huffy: "This gardener, this man, who is he? Surely he could come on a Monday or a Tuesday? One should not work on a Sunday. What sort of gardener is he?" Aunt Pauline was a righteous Christian and so, to her, Sundays were sacred.'

'Now, I have noticed,' Zachary continued, 'that the most outrageous excuses are often the least disputed. They disconcert the hearer. So Mother dug her heels in: "He works every day. He is *very* hard-working."'

'"And what do you call this gardener?" Aunt Pauline demanded.'

'"His name is Harman," Mother replied, grabbing the first name that came to mind. And there it was. Harman had a name. From that moment onwards, Harman *existed*.'

'Aunt Pauline muttered, "Harman, Harman … I've heard that name somewhere. I must know him, but I don't recall who he is … Where does he live?"'

'"He has never told me where he lives. If I want him, I leave a note at the Post Office," Mother improvised.'

'"I knew it!" Aunt Pauline exclaimed. "He has no home. He's a vagrant, a good-for-nothing, a swindler!" Making to leave, she added with vehemence: "You cannot trust such a man!" And there it was. From that moment onwards, Harman had a *character*.'

'And so you see,' concluded Zachary, with a self-satisfied grin, 'You cannot say he didn't exist!'

Amelie was unconvinced: 'What you mean, Uncle, is that he had an *imaginary* existence.'

Her uncle pounced on her words. 'Don't all the best of beings have an imaginary existence? It is not the most real of beings but the imaginary beings that exert the greatest influence on the human mind. Peace, freedom, democracy … everywhere and always, things with no greater claim to existence than Harman inspire nations with love and with hatred, with terror and hope and all manner of other things besides. Harman did all of this and just as well … I can prove it!'

Then, suspecting his point needed further support, he added, 'To *be* does not necessarily mean to be a physical thing. It only implies a *relation* to something beyond itself … to *us*, for example. Harman had relations aplenty. Tell her, Zoe. Defend Mr Harman from your daughter, who doubts his existence! Defend him from this injustice!'

Zoe laughed again, 'I'm sure Mr Harman was quite used to being treated unjustly.'

'Why? What happened?' Amelie asked.

'You really want to hear it?'

Amelie nodded. Her mother needed little encouragement. 'It was Aunt Pauline who started it. She declared Harman to be a vagrant, a drunkard, a robber. Yet she also reasoned that, since he was employed by my mother, who wasn't wealthy, he must be satisfied to work for pennies. So, thinking to replace her own gardener, who expected to be paid properly, she demanded that my mother send Harman to her. She waited in vain for Harman to come and then returned to accuse Mama of selfishness, of keeping Harman all to herself.'

'Now Mama stood accused, so she defended herself by pandering to her aunt's absurd beliefs about the character of Mr Harman: "I have not seen him again, dear Aunt. Perhaps he is in hiding." Of course that only provoked my Aunt, who became determined to get to the bottom of what had happened to him. She asked relatives, friends, neighbours and servants whether they knew of him. Surprisingly few were willing to admit they did not: "Mm, I've heard the name," said one; "Yes, I know him, but I don't know much about him," said another. The most detailed description came from her lawyer, who claimed that Harman had cut his lawns just days before.'

'Then, one morning, Aunt Pauline appeared unannounced at my father's office in a state of great excitement. "I have seen Harman! I have seen him!"'

'"Truly?" said Papa.'

'"Yes, without a doubt. A man of twenty, a low forehead, straw hair, squinty eyes …"'

'Papa was by nature a generous man: "It is true that your description could apply to Harman."'

'"You see! I knew it! I saw him! I called out to him, "Harman!" and he turned and looked at me. He has a bad face. You were careless to employ him. The rims of his ears were flat and that is a sure sign that he is a thief or an assassin — maybe worse!" She shuddered.'

'A few days later, some melons disappeared from Aunt Pauline's vegetable garden. The robber was not apparent, so she immediately suspected Harman. The police were called. They agreed that the robbery was committed by a single man, someone with the strength and dexterity to climb over a high wall and leave no footprints. The sergeant agreed: the robber could be none other than Harman. They knew all about Harman, it emerged, and had long been trying to get their hands on him to solve a spate of neighbourhood crimes. The local newspaper published a notice of the wanted criminal, with a description provided by the locals: a low forehead, straw hair, squinty eyes, sharp cheekbones, no rims on the ears.'

'It was then reported that Harman had been arrested and was in prison – though the prisoner was soon discovered to be a pedlar by the name of Smith, who was reluctantly released. Harman's whereabouts remained a mystery. He was starting to gain respect from the locals for his success in hiding himself, while being seen simultaneously in the town, in the fields, at the river's edge, on a boat … Being able to appear so suddenly at such diverse locations was a frightening, but awe-inspiring, skill.'

'But the best part was to come. One day, Aunt Pauline found her young cook in the kitchen unable to work, so distraught was she. Clearly some terrible calamity had befallen her. On questioning, the girl admitted that she had been secretly engaged to be married, but that her husband-to-be had abruptly abandoned her.'

'Aunt Pauline demanded to know the name of the cook's betrayer. The cook obstinately refused to name him. Aunt Pauline questioned everyone, but no-one knew who the culprit was. Finally she returned to the cook, demanding to be given the opportunity to challenge the scoundrel who had treated her so poorly. The cook remained stubbornly tight-lipped.'

'Suddenly a light switched on in Aunt Pauline's head: "It was Harman!" she cried. "Of course, why did I not realise? That miserable, *miserable* man!" The news that Harman had loved and left the cook shot through the neighbourhood at lightning speed. From the streetsweeper to the judge, everyone clearly saw the train of events and was filled with the greatest awe at the scandalous skills of the great Mr Harman.'

'And so this was the man we grew up with, who played in our childhood games, who hid our toys and rumpled the pages of our schoolbooks, whose voice was heard on the wind and whose eyes gleamed in the dead of night. He was a rogue, it was true ... but to us, he was more like a god.'

'For Papa, though, Harman was a philosophical character. Our father had great compassion for people. He did not think them entirely rational. Their mistakes, when they were not cruel, made him smile. I suspect he took belief in Harman as a model for all human beliefs. He always spoke of Harman as a real person, with merits and flaws like anyone else.'

'Mama would say, "You speak of him so seriously, when you know full well ..."'

'But Papa would interrupt her: "The entire neighbourhood believes in Harman. Would I be a good citizen to deny him? You must think twice before you deny an article of common faith." Yet he always took care to rule Harman out of his explanations of events in the town.'

'As for Mama, she reproached herself for giving birth to Harman, for he was purely a child of her invention – or so she thought.'

'One day, years later, my mother was talking with a friend when Harman's name came up somehow. "I met him once, you know," her friend mentioned.'

'"You met him?" Mama exclaimed. "What do you mean?"'

'"I met him at some function, years after he was accused of all those robberies and what-not ... a strange fellow, but harmless. I don't believe he was guilty of all the things he was accused of. You never met him?"'

'"No! No, never! But you're sure it was him?"'

'"Oh yes," her friend declared confidently. "He said his name was Harman. Besides, he fit the description: low forehead, straw hair, squinty eyes, sharp cheekbones ... that's him, isn't it?"'

'"Yes, but ... what ... how ...?" Mama dared not explain the truth to her friend after so many years of complete deception. And so she never learnt how a figure of her imagination had somehow taken human form.'

'Perhaps you are right, Zach. Perhaps the distance between

imaginary and other forms of existence is not as great as we suppose. Deep down, I am still very fond our dear Mr Harman. What an extraordinary man he was!'

WHAT DO YOU THINK?
QUESTIONS TO PONDER

What does it mean to exist? Is existence reserved for physical things alone or do non-physical things also 'exist'? If so, which non-physical things?

Is Zachery right to claim that imaginary things such as peace, freedom and democracy have as great – if not greater – claim to existence than physical things?

In what sense do the products of the imagination exist? Is it different from how physical things exist and, if so, how?

PHILOSOPHICAL CONUNDRUMS:
DO IMAGINARY BEINGS EXIST?

This story was written in the early 20th century by the celebrated French author, Anatole France. It was written as a light-hearted reflection on the human tendency to create imaginary scapegoats for various purposes: to explain things we cannot explain otherwise, to find a culprit when we wish to lay blame, to reinforce stereotypes of those we do not trust and so on.

The story also raises questions about Mr Harman's existence as an imaginary being. These are philosophical questions of reality and existence: what properly exists? How do we define 'existence'? What in the universe can we say exists in reality? These are questions of an area of philosophy called metaphysics, the study of the fundamental nature of being itself.

What exists? The question is so strikingly simple that you would think its answer should be equally so. But there is perhaps not a single question of philosophy that has produced such conflicting views – nor views held so tenaciously – as this. Here are some of these views.

The first view is one of the oldest and remains very popular. For something to exist, the Greek philosopher Aristotle claimed in the 4th century BC, it must have some sort of substance. What exactly Aristotle meant by 'substance' is unclear and what it should mean for us now is only marginally clearer. In recent times, philosophers have been happy to leave it to physicists to decide what 'substance' is, allowing that the definition will change over time, as physicists gain a better understanding of what there 'is'. For many philosophers, the best candidates for substantial existence are 'physical' or 'material' beings: to exist, a thing must be physical or material in some way. This theory takes different forms, with different names: we'll call it 'physicalism'.

The opposing view has also found many followers across the centuries. Plato objected to the idea that anything that comes into and passes out of existence could be held to exist, properly speaking. By its nature, 'existence' must describe things that are absolute and eternal, not things that merely happen to exist for a time in some random and variable way. The only candidate for ultimate existence that Plato could identify were the abstract ideas of things, which he called 'Forms'. A Form is effectively the essence of a thing: so, for example, what ultimately exists is 'redness', which is the essence of what all the red things in our world display. This theory is generally called 'idealism'.

There are other theories of existence, but one in particular deserves mention, because is the theory of Uncle Zachary in this story: existence is not defined by the identity of a thing in itself, but rather by its relations to other things. So, a chair exists, not because it is a physical thing, nor because it exhibits some ideal essence, but because it can be perceived or bumped into or sat upon by a person or a cat, or can bump another chair or … There are countless ways to identify its existence, but all concern its relations to other things that in turn exist due to their relations with it and other things – and so on.

How does Mr Harman fare in these theories? A physicalist would obviously not allow him to exist, nor any other imaginary beings: gods, ghosts, unicorns, Sherlock Holmes and so on. A physicalist might allow that imaginary things are significant or even important, especially since objects are often created in the imagination before becoming physical: helicopters, the Mona Lisa, *War and Peace*. He or she would nevertheless maintain that these things enter the realms of existence only when they become physical.

It may seem to you that this approach restricts what we normally want to be able to say about the existence of things. Consider Zachary's examples in this story: peace, freedom and democracy. Surely we need to grant these things existence in order to be able to discuss what goes on in this world. We want to be able to say that peace exists in a country – or not. Why not be able to say it? We certainly know what is meant in saying that these things do not exist, so why not grant them existence when they do? Why is the existence of a thing compromised by the fact that our word for it is an abstract, rather than a concrete, noun?

On Plato's approach, the ideals of peace, freedom and democracy exist because their existence explains the existence of the concrete things in this world that correspond to these ideals. On Zachary's approach, the ideals of peace, freedom and democracy exist because of their effect on those influenced by them. They exist because they are transformative: they shape cultures, they create to new ways of being. They exist as powerful forces, not merely in the imagination or in an ideal world, but also in reality. To rule them out of existence seems arbitrary.

But note that the 'objects' Zachary appeals to in his theory are, strictly speaking, *ideal,* rather than *imaginary,* objects. An idealist may well be inclined to draw a distinction here: admitting the existence of ideal beings doesn't commit us to the existence of imaginary beings. Plato in particular was deeply sceptical about the imaginary objects of art, for example. These, he placed at a lower level of existence even than physical objects, at a second order of remove from the ideal world of Forms. They imitate physical objects, which themselves imitate ideal objects or Forms.

Does it make sense to say that imaginary objects exist? Certainly, we make claims about imaginary beings that are true and false, just as we make claims of physical and ideal beings. To say that unicorns enjoy the company of thieves and bandits is to misunderstand the nature of unicorns, and this is so, even though there is no evidence of the physical existence of a unicorn. To say that Sherlock Holmes lived in Liverpool is to say something that is false, and this is so, even though Sherlock Holmes is an entity of fiction.

When we say, by contrast, that unicorns love those who are good and gentle, or that Holmes lived on Baker Street, London, we seem to imply the existence of unicorns and of Holmes. There seems something odd about attributing properties – rightly or wrongly – to things that don't exist. But if we do allow that imaginary things exist, in some sense, what sort of existence do they have? Presumably it would be a different form of existence than that of physical things. Zoe's response to the idea of Mr Harman's *actual* existence suggests that actual existence and imagined existence must indeed be different … but in what way, exactly?

CHAPTER SIX

HANS HECKLEBERRY'S LUCK

Hans Heckleberry had no luck at all. Now and then, you might hear someone say that they have no luck, but what they really mean to say is that their luck is bad and they're unhappy about it. So they do have some kind of luck after all, even if it is only bad luck. Almost everyone is like that. Almost everyone has luck of some kind, whether it be good or bad. But Hans Heckleberry's luck was not like that, since he had no luck at all. How he'd lost it, he had not the slightest idea – but lost it, he most certainly had.

He had a wife and child, which is generally considered good luck, yet they were not as robust and carefree as they might have been, which is generally considered bad. He was poor, which is bad luck, and yet his luck was not so very bad, since he always had enough to feed and clothe himself and his small family. He worked from dawn to dusk, and yet his luck was not so very good, because he never had one penny to lay on top of another.

Hans Heckleberry's wife was named Katharine. One evening, when Hans came into their cottage with enough money to buy bread and cheese but not a penny more, Katharine said, 'Hans Heckleberry, I do believe that you have no luck at all.'

'No,' said Hans, 'I have none.' And that was no more nor less than the truth.

'So what are you going to do about it?' asked Katharine.

'Nothing at all,' replied Hans.

'Nothing at all will put no meat on the table,' Katharine commented.

'It will take none away,' Hans observed. And that was no more nor less than the truth either.

'Why don't you go visit the wise woman in the woods and ask her what happened to your luck? Who knows, she may be able to tell you when and where you lost it.'

Hans was unconvinced: 'If I find my luck, it may be bad, not good. Then I would regret finding it.'

'Well, it may be worth looking for. If you find it and it doesn't look good, you can always leave it right there where you found it.'

'No, that won't do. When someone finds their luck, they're stuck with it, whether they like it or not.' That is what Hans said, but he had already made up his mind to go to the wise woman and ask about his luck. He merely argued with his wife to show that he thought her advice was not worth so very much ... so that then he could take it for nothing. Lots of people do that on occasion.

So, the next morning, Hans Heckleberry rose with the sun and headed out towards the woods. The air was sweet and fresh; the hedgerows were covered all over with white blossoms; the cuckoo was singing among the budding branches; the little flowers were looking up everywhere with their bright faces. Hans thought, 'If I find my luck on a day such as this, it must surely be good and not bad.'

After some time, he came to the cottage in the woods where lived the wise woman who knew a great many things. He took off his hat and smoothed down his clothes and then rapped timidly on the door.

'Hans Heckleberry, my good man,' said the wise woman, 'come in, come in.' She was the strangest woman that you might ever see. Her face was grey with age, her hair as white as snow. Her eyes were silver and twinkled brightly. She wore a long grey robe over her shoulders and had a black cat sitting on her lap. It was as if, when colour was distributing itself across the universe, it had somehow passed her by.

'Now, what might you be wanting, Hans Heckleberry?' asked the wise woman.

'I'd like to find my luck, if I may,' said Hans.

'That all depends … Where did you lose it, Hans Heckleberry?' said she.

'That I do not know,' said he.

'Hmmm,' said the wise woman thoughtfully. Hans said nothing at all.

After a while, she spoke again. 'Do you have enough to eat and drink?' said she.

'Oh yes,' said Hans.

'Do you have clothes for your family?' said she.

'Oh yes,' said Hans.

'Are you warm and comfortable in winter?' said she.

'Oh yes,' said Hans.

'Then you should leave well enough alone,' she declared, 'since luck can give you nothing more.'

'It might give me money in my pocket,' said Hans.

'And it might take the food from your table and the clothes from your back,' said she.

'All the same, I should like to find it again. It's mine, after all. If I can just lay my hands on it, I might be able to turn it to some good, even if it is bad.'

'I doubt that,' said the wise woman.

Nevertheless, she saw that, for good or ill, Hans was set on finding his luck and nothing she said would change that. So she handed Hans the black cat, which hissed at him, and heaved herself out of her chair and limped over to her closet and brought out a great book. She set it down on her table – thump! – and opened it at the middle with her thumb and then turned the pages slowly, until finally she stopped and ran her fingers up and down some columns of dense script.

'Hans Heckleberry,' she said finally, 'your luck fell out of your pocket three years ago, along with a silver coin. The coin is long gone, but the luck is still sitting there, on a rock at the crossroads, between the road that goes to your cottage and the one that goes to the fair.' So saying, she shut her book – thump! – and put it away in the closet.

Then she went to a chest and pulled out a small pouch. 'When you have found your luck, be careful to put it in this little bag and do not let it out. No evil spirit can escape this bag, so long as you pull the strings tight. And now, I bid good day to you, Hans Heckleberry.'

Hans slipped the pouch into his pocket and set out for the crossroads. When he got there, he looked here and there, this way and that, but for a long time he could see nothing at all. After much searching, he saw a tiny black beetle running hither and thither across the rock.

'I wonder whether this can be my luck,' thought Hans, catching the beetle between his thumb and finger – but carefully, since he did not want to squash it. He prized it off the rock – pop! – and then held it tight. Looking more closely, he saw a nasty-looking little imp, kicking and squirming and rolling its red eyes in such a horrible manner that it gave Hans the fright of his life and he almost dropped it. He stuffed it into the pouch and pulled the strings very tight.

So now Hans Heckleberry knew full well what his luck was like.

Anyone would've thought that Hans would leave well enough alone. Now that had his luck tied safely in the pouch, however, he began to feel more confident. What harm could there be in seeing what sort of bargain he might make with his luck?

'What will you do for me if I let you out?' asked he.

'Nothing at all,' snarled his luck.

'We'll see about that,' said Hans and he hid the pouch at the back of a cupboard and let it sit there for a few weeks.

Then he went to the pouch again. 'What will you do for me if I let you out?' asked he.

'Nothing at all,' snarled his luck.

'We'll see about that,' said Hans and he put the pouch back in the cupboard and let it sit there for a few days longer.

Every few days, Hans went to his luck, to see what sort of bargain he could strike. His luck said nothing … and so the weeks passed. Then, at last, his luck gave in.

'Hans, Hans,' said his luck one morning, 'if you let me out of this nasty old bag, I'll give you a thousand silver coins.'

'No, no,' said Hans. 'Coins are only coins. They slip through your fingers, until nothing is left of them. I won't trust my luck for that!'

'Hans, Hans,' said his luck the following morning, 'if you let me out of this nasty old bag, I'll give you two thousand silver coins.'

'No, no,' said Hans. 'Two thousand coins do exactly the same as one thousand coins, only more slowly. I won't trust my luck for that either!'

'Then, what will it take to let me out, Hans Heckleberry?' asked his luck.

'Over in the field is my old plough,' said Hans. 'Every time I plough a furrow, at the end of the furrow, I want to find a golden nugget. If not, well, it's the back of the cupboard for you!'

'Done!' said Hans' luck.

'Done!' said Hans.

He opened his pouch, out jumped his luck and – puff! – it disappeared. Hans never saw his luck again with his mortal eyes, but he heard the words that luck cried out, as it disappeared from view: 'You've made a bad bargain, Hans Heckleberry, that I can tell you!' And that was no more nor less than the truth.

Hans Heckleberry did not wait to try out his luck, as you may guess. Off he went like the wind to borrow his neighbour's grey horse. He fastened the horse to the plough and dug the first furrow. When he had come to the end of it – bump! – he came upon a golden nugget. Hans looked at it as though he would swallow it with his eyes. He dug another furrow and – bump! – he came upon another golden nugget. So he went on all day, digging furrows and striking golden nuggets until his pockets were brimming with gold.

Yet, you see, bad luck had the best of the bargain in the end. For, from that day forwards, Hans did not know a moment of peace and calm. All he did was plough, plough, plough … morning, noon and night. Only frost and darkness kept him from his labours. His friends thought he had gone crazy and laughed at him whenever they saw him in the street: 'Hans Heckleberry, what are you doing here? Why aren't you at your plough?' His family grew tired of his obsession and stopped talking to him, leaving him alone.

When he was not ploughing, Hans would sit and brood about some quicker way of doing his ploughing, for it seemed to him that his gold nuggets came in very slowly. He blamed himself for not having asked his luck for three gold nuggets at the end of each furrow – or six or ten – rather than a pitiful one. He took no comfort in his gathering wealth. As each day passed, as the chests of gold nuggets piled up in his cellar, he grew more haggard and worn. He told no-one how rich he was, for fear that someone would come and steal his riches away from him. When he was not ploughing for gold, he spent his time counting his pennies and watching over them fearfully. Such was the way Hans Heckleberry spent his days.

When Hans finally went the way all of us must eventually go, his heirs found the chests of gold in his cellar and they bought lands, became gentlemen and were very pleased with themselves altogether. Whether that brought them happiness, who can say? We do know that it brought none to Hans Heckleberry. Since none of his heirs knew where the gold had come from, no thanks did Hans receive from them. They put it all down to luck. And that was, indeed, no more nor less than the truth.

WHAT DO YOU THINK?
QUESTIONS TO PONDER

Is there such a thing as good or bad luck? What sort of things can luck get you – or not get you?

Was Hans Heckleberry right to go out in search of his luck? Should he have left well enough alone?

Why do you think Hans Heckleberry was no longer happy, after he had made his deal with luck?

PHILOSOPHICAL CONUNDRUMS: WHAT BRINGS HAPPINESS?

There are several stories in this volume that come from the great American writers, collectors and illustrators of children's tales and fairy stories, Howard and Katharine Pyle. At the turn of the 20th century, the Pyle family were responsible for a vast treasure trove of such literature, published in many volumes.

Is there any such thing as luck? If there is, it seems that, by its very nature, it must be unevenly distributed across the population: if everyone were lucky, we wouldn't think of it as luck, but simply the norm. Does that imply that some people are lucky while others are not? If so, why might that be? Do people create their own luck or are some people naturally lucky? And does luck always lead to happiness or could luck, as in this story, be a mixed blessing to those it 'favours'?

The idea of luck is bound up with notions of fate and fortune: are some people fated to do well in life and others to do poorly? The earliest literary sources – which we will explore later in this book – tell of heroes and heroines fated by the gods to suffer through no fault of their own. The authors of these stories appear to have believed that we are all subject to fate and that its impact is erratic, inexplicable and often catastrophic. Modern thought, by contrast, tends in the other direction, suggesting that our fate is ultimately our own to decide, regardless of the social, political, religious and other influences that impact upon us. Perhaps the truth is somewhere between these two.

Now, if we want to analyse this concept of luck with any degree of precision, the first thing we would expect is to be able to define it: what, exactly, is luck? One way of doing this might be to decide on particular instances of luck and then determine what they have in common that makes them all examples of 'luck'. The story above makes clear, however, that whether you see something as lucky depends on your description of it. Is Hans lucky to have food for his family or unlucky to have nothing more? Likewise, is someone lucky to have survived two plane crashes or unlucky to have found themselves in two crashing planes in the first place? The difficulty of identifying instances of luck is telling: how are we to define 'luck', much less analyse it, if it is not even apparent to us when it exists?

Another approach might be to decide on an exemplary instance of luck and then determine what it is about this instance – its essential or defining feature – that makes it such a good example of 'luck'. Here, most people would offer an example like winning the lottery, where something lucky happens to us that is entirely beyond our control. Winning the lottery is lucky, we think, precisely because we have so little hand in it.

Yet here again, our example does not bring clarity, because we also correlate luck with the size of the risks we take. We are more likely to think of someone who returns from a trip to the Moon as lucky than someone who returns from a trip to the local shops. But the choice to go to the Moon or to the shops is surely ours to make, which suggests that luck lies within our control after all. We can control the extent of our luck by controlling our exposure to situations which require it. This is exactly what the wise woman of this story notes, when she warns Hans of the risks of going out to find his luck.

Again, it appears we have no clear sense of what luck is. And again, we have an example of how philosophy leads us to doubt what we thought we knew or what we took for granted. While we naturally assume that luck exists and that some people are lucky, our inability to define 'luck' reflects our inability to determine where – or even *whether* – luck exists. Perhaps there is simply no such thing as luck – or perhaps questions of luck have simply not yet received the philosophical attention they deserve.

There are further questions in this story, however, that have received a *great* deal of philosophical attention. These questions –

'What is happiness?' and 'What makes for happiness in life?' – lead us back to the Greek philosopher, Aristotle, whom we met in the last chapter. Aristotle's contribution to the history of philosophy is colossal, not least because of his analysis of these very questions regarding happiness.

In his *Ethics*, Aristotle starts from the point we left off in the attempt to define 'luck': he notes that, while all things aim for happiness, there is no agreed definition of what happiness is. He therefore tries a different approach: he searches for something in the concept of happiness itself which may enlighten us as to what it truly is. To the modern mind, Aristotle's reasoning is obscure, but its conclusion is by no means unexpected.

First, Aristotle claims that what a thing aims for is the good of the thing itself: it makes little sense to say that a thing should aim for what is not good for it. This much is surely debatable, but no more so that his second claim, which is that the good of a thing must be the best of which that thing is capable – the highest ability that defines the thing and distinguishes it from others. This makes sense in that we cannot know what is good for a thing unless we know what that thing does. His third claim reminds us that Aristotle is a philosopher first and foremost: the highest ability of humans – that which defines us and sets us apart from other animals – is the ability to reason. It follows, then, that human happiness lies in the pursuit of reason. It lies in philosophy.

This may sound like a recipe for bookishness, but it is not. For reason governs not merely our intellectual activities, but all our endeavours. It is the source of right actions. Our natural inclination is to allow our desires to direct our actions – for good or ill. When we subject these desires to reason, however, we seek what is good and virtuous. This is the course that leads to happiness, says Aristotle.

Subjecting our desires to reason, for Aristotle, means plotting a course between competing forms of excess, adopting what is called the 'golden mean', by which he meant a form of moderation or temperance. So, for example, Hans' happiness is blighted when he adopts one form of excess – meanness or miserliness – to the complete exclusion of its opposite –

extravagance or profligacy. His happiness would have been better served by balancing these two opposing vices, to reach the golden mean of generosity or liberality. Is this a fair assessment of what went wrong for Hans, do you think? Did he lose his reason when luck favoured him? Is luck somehow like this: a foil to reason? Is the happiness we expect from luck somehow unfounded?

A true philosopher, Aristotle maintained that happiness is found in the pursuit of reason, above all else. Is this fair? Would reason have led Hans to tame his desires? Are the emotions properly subject to reason in this way? Or is it possible that Aristotle himself created an imbalance between opposites, in allowing reason to dominate emotion so thoroughly? Does reason always prescribe what is good and virtuous, do you think? Does it inevitably bring happiness, do you think, or might it also sometimes lead in the other direction?

Chapter Seven

The Apple of Contentment

Years ago, when people's lives were simpler than they are these days, there lived in a cottage between the hills a woman and her three daughters. The first daughter had a large round face and sleepy green eyes, and her mother loved her like a river loves the rain, since she too had a large round face and sleepy green eyes. The second daughter had a pointy nose and long lank hair, and her mother loved her like a forest loves the trees, since she too had a pointy nose and long lank hair. The third daughter had dark playful eyes and unruly black hair, but the mother loved her not at all, since she had neither dark playful eyes nor unruly black hair. So it is with some people.

The first sister dressed in her finest clothes every day and never did a stitch of work, for fear of getting her fine clothes dirty. The second sister sat around all day and never lifted a finger, for fear of tiring herself out. Meanwhile the third daughter dressed in the plainest clothes and drove the geese through the hills in the morning and home again in the evening, so that they might feed on the young grass and grow fat and fetch a good price at the market. Her name was Sophia but, to the people in the hills, she was known as the Goose Girl and loved by them for being sweet, merry, kind and good.

One morning, Sophia started off through the hills with her flock of geese as usual. She wandered along the dusty road until she came to a valley where a bridge crossed a rambling stream. There, on the branch of an alder tree which hung over the stream, was a dear little red cap with a shiny silver bell sewn onto its tip. Sophia looked this way and that for its owner, but she saw no-one. So she took the cap off the branch and put it in her pocket, thinking to sew another just like it, since it was so delightful.

Off she went once again with her geese. Hardly had she gone a dozen paces, however, when she heard a voice calling out to her: 'Sophia! Sophia! Hold on a minute!' She looked around and who should she see but an odd little man, no more than the height of her knees, dressed in a red jacket and green trousers. He had a head of grey hair and long grey beard reaching down to the tips of his pointy green shoes.

Now, Sophia knew a thing or two about gnomes, as did everyone who lived in those hills. 'What is it?' she replied, all innocence, though of course she knew exactly what the little man wanted. The man, it transpired, had been fishing for tiddlers in the stream when a puff of wind blew his cap into the water. He had managed to retrieve it and hung it out on the branch to dry. Would Sophia please give the cap to the gnome?

Well, yes, of course Sophia would give the cap to the gnome … but the sight of him had somehow put her in a playful mood. Sophia guessed that the little man might have a trick up his tiny sleeves and she wondered just what it might be. A little good-natured teasing would surely not hurt him.

And so she replied, 'And what will you give me for the cap?' Well, the man said he would give her five guineas.

'Is that all your cap is worth?' Sophia laughed. Well, then, the man would give her one hundred guineas.

'I don't want your money,' the girl laughed good-naturedly, knowing full well that a gnome's coins have a habit of disappearing as soon as they pass from a gnome's hands into your own.

'Well, then, I will give you this,' said the man, handing her a small black seed. 'That there,' he declared, 'is a seed from the apple of contentment. Plant it and it will grow into a tree. From the tree will grow an apple. Everyone who sees the apple will long for it, but no-one in the world will be able to pick it but you. And when you eat from the tree, you will be content. I give this to you since I know you are kind and good. And since you are kind and good, will you now please give me my cap?'

Well, yes, of course she would ... Sophia would certainly give him the cap for a seed such as that!

As soon as the man had his cap, he popped it on his head and took off like the wind, disappearing into a hole in the hill. Sophia put the seed in her pocket and went on her way with her geese, so that they might feed on the young grass in the hills. That night, before she went to bed, Sophia planted the seed from the apple of contentment in the ground outside her window.

The next morning, when she awoke, the light streaming through her bedroom window seemed somehow mottled. She crept out of bed, tiptoed to the window and there, for all the world to see, was a big, beautiful apple tree. Sure enough, on the tree hung a single apple which shone in the sun as if it were made of gold. Sophia reached over and plucked the apple just as easily as if it were a gooseberry. Another appeared instantly in its place. And when she ate the apple, it tasted as if it were made of sunlight. Sophia felt as if a great burst of sunshine was warming every bone of her body, down into the depths of her soul. A big, broad smile lit up her face.

By and by, the oldest sister came out of the house and saw the tree. She saw, too, the apple hanging from the tree and she wanted it for herself ... but thinking that something *might* be so does not make it so. She grabbed and she grasped for the apple, but she might as well have been grasping for the sun, for all her success.

After a while, out came the second sister and saw the tree. She saw, too, the apple hanging from the tree and wanted it just as much as the oldest sister ... but thinking that something *should* be so does not make it so. She clambered and she climbed over the tree, but she might as well have been climbing to the moon, for all her success.

Then, last of all, out came the mother and saw the tree. She saw, too, the apple hanging from the tree and wanted it just as much as her elder daughters ... but thinking that something *must* be so does not make it so. She tugged and she tore at the branches, but she could no more tear the apple from the tree than she could tear the stars from the sky.

All they could do was to stand under the tree and wish for the apple. The longer they stood, the more they longed for it, as they had longed for nothing else in their lives. They are not the only ones to have done such a thing. The apple of contentment is often found to hang just beyond one's reach.

Now, it happened later that day that a queen came riding along the dusty road with all her court. Passing the cottage, she looked up and saw the apple hanging from the tree. Suddenly, a great desire came upon her to taste it. She called out to one of her servants to go to the cottage and ask whether she might have the apple. The servant went to the door. Would the mother please give the apple to the queen?

Well, yes, of course she would … for a purse of gold, the queen was most welcome to it. The servant paid the purse of gold and went to pluck the apple. He grabbed and he grasped, but it was no use. The servant had to go back to the queen and admit that, although the queen had bought the apple, he could no more grasp it than he could grasp the sun.

So the queen told her steward to pluck the apple. The steward went. He clambered and he climbed, but it was no use, for he could no more climb to it than she could climb to the moon.

Eventually, the queen lost patience and decided to pluck the apple herself. She tugged and tore at the branches but, in the end, she had to admit that the apple was simply not to be had. She went home feeling strangely discontented.

Over the next few days, the queen could think of nothing but the apple. She found herself dreaming of the apple as soon as she closed her eyes at night. She found herself talking of the apple to anyone who would listen. The more she could not have it, the more she wanted it. So it is with some people.

So the queen sought the counsel of the wise woman who lived in the highest tower at the furthest end of the palace. The wise woman told her that the only person who can pluck the fruit of contentment is the one to whom the tree belongs … and the tree belonged to the daughter of the woman in the cottage.

The queen was thrilled to hear the wise woman's words. She gathered her court and hurried back to the cottage. The woman was home with her elder daughters, as usual, while Sophia was away in the hills with her geese. The queen wished to know about the daughter who owned the tree. Would the daughter please give the apple to the queen?

Well, yes, of course she would … but the girl would need to scramble up the tree and she would not do that in front of all the court. Let the queen go home and the daughter would bring the apple to the queen in good time.

As soon as the queen had gone, her mother sent for Sophia and told her she must pluck the apple for the queen. The oldest daughter took the apple and wrapped it in a napkin and set off to the palace and presented herself before all the court. Had she bought the apple?

Well, yes, of course she had … all wrapped in a fine napkin. She opened the napkin, but there was nothing in the napkin but an old stone. So she was sent home with nothing but the queen's stony glare.

Then the Queen sent her steward to the cottage. Again, the woman was home with her two elder daughters, while Sophia was away in the hills with her geese. The steward wished to know about the daughter who owned the tree. Was there another daughter? Would that daughter please give the apple to the queen?

Well, yes, of course she would … but the girl would need to wrestle with the tree and she would not do that in front of the steward. Let the steward go home and the daughter would bring the apple to the queen in good time.

As soon as the steward had gone, her mother sent for Sophia and told her she must pluck a second apple for the queen. The second daughter took the apple and wrapped it in a napkin and set off to the palace and presented herself before the court. Had she bought the apple?

Well, yes, of course he had … all wrapped in a fine napkin. She opened the napkin, but there was nothing in the napkin but a clod of earth. So she was sent home with nothing but the queen's earthy insults.

After a while the queen sent her servant to the cottage where the woman lived. Again the woman was home with her two older daughters, while Sophia was away in the hills with her geese. The servant wished to know about the daughter who owned the tree. Was there another daughter?

Well yes, but the third daughter was a poor, ragged thing, of no account, good for nothing in the world but to take the geese to the hills. Yes, that was all well and good, but would she please give the apple to the queen?

Well, yes, of course she would ... so there was nothing for the mother to do but to send to the hills for Sophia. Soon she came and plucked the apple just as easily as if it were a gooseberry. Then the servant made a deep bow to her, for he saw that it was she that they had been looking for all along.

Sophia slipped the apple into her pocket and set off with the servant to the palace and presented herself before the court. Had she bought the apple?

Well, yes, of course she had ... and Sophia gave the apple to the queen. Right there, in front of all the court, the queen took a great bite of the apple and a big, broad smile lit up her face. Then she looked at Sophia and thought she had never seen such a sweet, charming and adorable young woman in all the days of her life. Would Sophia please come to live at the palace with the queen and all her court?

Well, yes, of course she would ... Who wouldn't?

Sophia's mother was outraged: how could a queen prefer the company of the Goose Girl to that of her elder daughters? 'Never mind,' she said to herself. 'We still have the tree, even if we cannot eat from it.' But no; they had nothing of the kind. For the next morning, there stood the tree outside the window of Sophia's room at the palace. This was a good thing for the queen, of course, for she needed a taste of the apple every now and then, and there was no-one to pick it for her but Sophia.

And so did the apple give Sophia the contentment she had been promised for being kind and good ... and, for that matter, the queen as well?

Well, yes, of course it did ... They were the happiest two people between the sun and the moon and all the stars that shone above them. For nobody in the world can have more than contentment … and that was precisely what the apple had brought them.

What do you think?
Questions to ponder

The story suggests that Sophia is rewarded for being good and kind, but does goodness always reap a reward? If not, is there any reason to be good?

What did the wise woman mean when she said that the only person who can pluck the fruit of contentment is the one to whom the tree belongs?

Is it true that nobody in the world can have more than contentment? Should we strive for more?

Philosophical conundrums: why be good?

This story repeats an idea we saw in the last chapter: happiness is not to be found in excess, but in moderation. Here, happiness consists in contentment, which is found in a simple, honest life, at peace with oneself, with others and with the world around us. Happiness is a reward that comes to us as a result of leading a good life. The questions that arise here lie in a branch of philosophy called ethics, the study of how we should act, the study of good action.

The theme of the rewards that are due to those who are good is common in fairy tales and in children's literature in general. Much of this literature has a moral tone: it is designed to help children understand the benefits of good conduct. Sophia is good in that she is gentle, hard-working, uncomplaining and generous. She deserves the good that comes to her because she is herself good.

(The teasing of the gnome is forgivable because gnomes are rogues and so can expect to be teased. Anyway, it shows that Sophia is not entirely compliant.) The story is unusual among fairy tales in dispensing with the other side of the moral counterweight: the punishments due to those who are not good. Fairy stories are full of violent punishments awarded to evildoers – stepmothers and stepsisters in particular.

From a literary perspective, the resolution of a story by the balancing of moral forces – the balancing of good and evil – is satisfying. We expect a story to provide a satisfactory resolution of this kind. The idea that fate has a role to play in restoring the balance of good and evil in the universe is deeply embedded in our literary sense. If evil were rewarded and good punished, what would be the point of the story?

From a philosophical perspective, things are not so simple. First of all is the question of fact: is it true that good is rewarded and evil punished in this world? It does not take long to discover that the laws of the universe are not as fair as fairy tales suggest – which may of course explain their appeal in the first place. Is there any connection at all between the good we do in the world and the good that comes back to us – if indeed it ever does? Is there any reason to expect that good is rewarded? Do we truly reap what we sow?

Religions have a good deal to say on this subject. Western religions promise that, in the end, there is inevitably a balancing of good and evil. If a cosmic settlement does not come in this life, it will come later, when God judges us and rewards us in heaven or punishes us in hell. Eastern religions likewise promote the idea of cosmic balance. The idea of karma ensures that the good you do in this life is rewarded in a later, better, life in the great cycle of reincarnation.

These may be abstract philosophical and religious ideas, but they have a practical effect: ideas of good and evil influence how people behave. There is surely a deterrent from doing evil if you know we will pay for it in the afterlife. For those who do not believe in an afterlife, however, it is difficult to square the idea of moral forces at work in the universe with the idea that the good receive no reward in this life. If good goes unrewarded, then what is the point of being good?

In the last chapter, we considered Aristotle's claim that happiness comes from a life of reason, where reason prescribes a path between the two opposing forces: between rashness and cowardice, for example, or between vanity and humility. Upon this approach, goodness and happiness exist in accord with each other, and good action is justified not merely in its own terms – in that it is prescribed by reason – but also by the happiness it brings with it.

One of the merits of Aristotle's approach is that, by defining the 'good' as the highest of which we as a species are capable, the 'good' can be interpreted in communal, rather than in individual, terms. For Aristotle, man is a social animal: society comes before the individual. So, while there is little evidence that individuals invariably reap the rewards owed to them for good actions, perhaps, as a society, we reap the rewards of the good actions of the members of our society. Studies show that organisations that promote kindness and generosity amongst their members are more likely to thrive and to be productive, and less likely to fail during a downturn, than those which encourage selfishness and exploitation. Is this evidence that goodness receives a reward at a social, if not at an individual, level?

Another advantage of thinking of the good in communal, rather than individual, terms is that it helps to explain the actions of those who sacrifice their own happiness for that of others. Such individuals become role models for society because of the good they bring to it by their selflessness. An Aristotelian approach may show that those who sacrifice themselves for society derive happiness from the knowledge of the good they do. This may account for the contentment of our heroine in this story, whose selflessness contributes to the good of those around her.

While it may be pleasing to think that it is so, it is at least arguable that societies as a whole are just as liable to suffer unjustly as the individuals within it. Is our analysis of social goods merely an attempt to salvage the idea of cosmic balance, against all evidence to the contrary? If there is no guarantee that good is rewarded, either at an individual or social level, might this be because there is in fact nothing in the universe that is good or bad of itself? There may be no cosmic balance precisely because there are no moral forces in existence that require balancing.

The idea that good and evil exist in the world is deeply embedded in our ways of thinking, so much so that it is hard to think otherwise. It is hard to imagine that good and evil are not part of the natural order of things. The 19th century German philosopher Friedrich Nietzsche caused something of a philosophical scandal when he claimed that there is nothing that is good or evil in itself. Good and evil, he maintained, are merely value judgements we make about whether we *like* certain ideas, certain forms of behaviour, certain ways of being and so on – or not. Perhaps we say that an action is good simply as a way of making ourselves feel good when we perform that action.

Nietzsche's analysis does not necessarily mean that we shouldn't be good. There may still be reasons to act with kindness or justice towards our neighbours. We just need to clarify what these reasons are and how they justify our actions. Nietzsche was pointing out, among other things, that what we think is good is open to change. Western societies once held homosexuality to be evil, but slavery, not so; now most quite reasonably maintain the opposite. Are there any goods that are good for all people for all time? The question whether there are any goods that are good for all people for all time is an interesting one to ponder. Whether these goods are part of the moral fabric of the universe itself is perhaps even more so.

CHAPTER EIGHT

THE GOOD NEIGHBOUR

Long ago, there was a farmer who lived in a remote region of Norway. His farm was of a good size, so he should have been able to make a good living, yet he had nothing but bad luck with his cattle. They would wander into the river to drink and be swept away by a sudden surge, or stand in the middle of a field and be struck by a stray bolt of lightning, or succumb to some mysterious disease of which the vet had never heard and for which there was no name. And so his farm was not a success.

At last, the farmer's luck became so bad that he feared he would lose everything he had. Despairing of making anything of this property, he sold it and moved to a new location, in a valley deep in the wildwood, far from the old one and even further from civilisation. There he planned to make a new life for himself with greater success.

The farmer's new property was wild and windswept, but it presented him with all the opportunities he could possibly want. There was no-one living around about him at all but, being a solitary soul, the farmer was unconcerned. He had his beloved dog and a herd of contented cows for company. The dog was increasingly playful and happy with their new home and the cows were calm and docile, relishing the fresh pastures. As the days went by, his property proved itself more productive than the one they had left behind. Not a single cow wandered off, was struck by lightning, nor stricken by an unknown and unnamed disease. Thus the farmer was happy.

Given the property's seclusion, it was a surprise to him when, one day, he met someone on the rough pathway which ran along the edge of the forest to his property.

'Good day, neighbour!' the person addressed him, pleasantly enough.

'Good day,' replied the farmer. 'I thought I was all alone here in this valley. Are you a neighbour of mine?'

'Yes, I am. You can see my homestead over there, can you not?' the neighbour inquired quizzically. 'After all, it is not so far from your own.' The farmer looked in the direction his neighbour was pointing and there lay a farmhouse he had never seen before, solid, sturdy and handsome.

The farmer had little trouble discerning that this must be one of the underground people of whom he had heard whispers. Until this moment, he had not believed such people existed. He had always understood the underground people to be like fairies, only perhaps a little larger, or like goblins, only perhaps a little smaller. Studying the individual in front of him, the farmer guessed that this person must be of a different nature again. Whether imp, sprite, elf, pixie, gnome or indeed human, he simply could not say. Yet he had no fear, since the person appeared to be gentle and friendly.

So the farmer invited his neighbour to share a jug of mead and the neighbour seemed happy to accept the invitation. They talked of this and that and a little more besides. Evening followed afternoon and the farmer brought out a simple meal of meat and cheese. Before long, it was time for the neighbour to be making his farewells. As he was doing so, he turned to the farmer earnestly and said, 'Listen here, there is one thing you must do for me.'

'Of course, if it is within my power, just let me know what it is.'

'You must move your cowshed. It is in my way,' was the answer.

The farmer was taken aback. 'No, I'll not do that,' he replied warily. 'I put the cowshed up just weeks ago. Winter will soon be upon us and what would I do with my cattle then, if the new cowshed were not ready?'

The neighbour cocked his head to the side and looked at the farmer intently. He appeared to be saddened, rather than offended, by the farmer's words. 'Well, do as you choose,' he said, 'but, if you do not move your cowshed, things cannot not go well for you here.' And with that, he thanked the farmer for his kind hospitality and was on his way.

The farmer was astounded by the turn of events. His neighbour may have been different from others he'd had in the past, but that had not seemed to matter. He had appeared so … well, *neighbourly*. The farmer had no intention of carrying out his request: it would be reckless to tear down his new cowshed with the long winter approaching. He would lose his cows if he did not have somewhere warm and safe for them to pass the long winter months. Besides, it would be so much hard work. So the farmer ignored his neighbour's advice and did nothing.

Then, one afternoon, as the sun was setting behind the forest, the farmer was standing in his cowshed, sharing a quiet conversation with his cows, when suddenly he felt the earth start to give way underneath his feet. He felt himself sinking slowly and steadily into the ground beneath him. He tried to prevent himself from falling by grabbing on to one of the cows, but cows are slippery creatures and present little that is handy to cling on to. So down and down he went, until he found himself landing on soft earth below. He was standing in an underground house.

The room in which the farmer had arrived so unexpectedly was pleasant: everything was handsome and designed with an eye for simple charm. The space was large and open, with furniture that was solid and well-crafted, and fittings that were neat and homely. Everything about it suggested a comfortable country lifestyle for its residents.

As he got up and patted himself down, he came face to face with his neighbour, who was standing by, clearly expecting his arrival. The neighbour welcomed him and introduced him to his companions, who were sitting on benches around a great wooden table the stood in the centre of the room.

His neighbour invited him to take a seat on one of the benches. Still confused by his sudden dislocation, the farmer made himself comfortable. His host talked of this and that, and a little more besides, as if sitting in an underground room were entirely normal – as indeed it would be for you, if it were your home. Before long, food was brought out on silver platters and drink in silver jugs.

The farmer was invited to take a plate and a mug and fill them with whatever he chose.

There he sat in the company of his neighbours, all talking to each other in an animated way and gesturing to him to eat. He took some food on his plate and some drink in his mug. The food was beautifully prepared and looked and smelt delicious. The drink appeared to be cheering. The farmer was starting to overcome his surprise and feel rather warmly towards the dinner party, despite the unexpected manner of his invitation to it.

So, imagine his alarm when, entirely without warning, just as he was about to take the first bite of his food, something fell from above and landed with a thump and a splatter near his plate. It had plainly come from the cowshed above and, what was worse, it had plainly come from one of the cows themselves. The smell alone quite put him off his meal. The farmer looked up to the ceiling to see whether anything further would be dropping into his meal and narrowly missed being sprayed by another deposit.

The farmer turned to his host in horror.

'Yes, yes,' said the neighbour, not in the least surprised by the disruption to their meal. 'You see how it is? We never eat in peace. As soon as we sit down to eat, we are deluged from above by dirt and straw and goodness knows what else besides. No matter how hungry we are, we cannot enjoy our dinner. It really is a very great shame,' he lamented.

The farmer did not know what to say.

'Now, if you were to do us the favour of setting up your cowshed elsewhere,' continued the neighbour, 'I do believe it would be best for all of us. We will enjoy our meals in peace once again and I do believe your cows will always do the same. If you do not, I fear … well …' The neighbour seemed reluctant to finish his thought.

The farmer needed no further persuasion. The following day, he went straight to work pulling down his shed and putting it up again in another place entirely. But he cannot have worked alone in this, for at night as he slept, the building of the cowshed continued at a brisk pace. And this is indeed what they say: many hands make light work. The task was by no means as onerous as the farmer had expected.

Nor did the farmer regret his decision for a moment. From the day he moved his cattle into the new shed, the hay bins at the end of the shed were always well-stocked. The cows were always content and keen to converse with him at the end of the day. And so the farmer was happy.

A farmer's life is seldom entirely free from care. There was once a year of terrible scarcity, when feed was short across the country and farmers everywhere were having to slaughter their cattle and sell their farmlands. In the midst of this calamity, the farmer arrived at his cowshed one morning to find his dog missing, the cows along with him, and the young calves besides. Yet so trusting had the farmer become in the protection of his neighbour, he suspected that the cows had been taken to pasture on his neighbours' lands and he did not fear their loss.

Sure enough, it was just as he suspected. Towards the spring, when the woods became green and the skylarks sang once again, there was the dog on the pathway which ran along the edge of the forest, barking and leaping, and after him followed the cows and the calves, now almost fully grown. The whole herd was so fat and contented that it was a joy to welcome them home again and to have them back in the cowshed for a quiet conversation as the evenings lengthened.

The farmer's heart was filled with warmth and gratitude towards his gentle neighbour and he hoped to return the hospitality he and his cows had received. The chance to thank his neighbour in person never presented itself, however … for, from the day of his invitation to the underground dinner party, the farmer never set eyes on his neighbour again.

What do you think?
Questions to ponder

Should we be good to our neighbours because it is good for us or because it is good for our neighbours?

Are the interests of humans and the interests of other living things aligned? If not, should the interests of humans prevail?

Is it right for humans to rule over nature, do you think?

Philosophical Conundrums: Why Care for the Environment?

This unusual tale is found in a collection of Norwegian folk tales, collected early in the last century. The idea of small people who live in hills or underground is a common theme of European folklore, as is the ability of these people to influence your luck, for good or ill. The unusual aspect of this particular story is the opportunity given to the farmer to negotiate his arrangements with his neighbour. In many such stories, the relationship between human actions and magical reactions is less easily explained.

I use this simple story to introduce the theme, widespread in folkloric traditions, that human action occurs within a larger natural environment which includes an array of other beings, each with concerns and interests that must be respected for the good of all. This simple idea may appear somewhat obvious to the modern mind, but it is surprising how rare it is in our various traditions, outside of folklore.

Western religious traditions, for example, emerged from the worldview of Genesis 1, the first book of the Old Testament, in which mastery over all living things was expressly given by God to humans: 'Rule over the fish in the sea and the birds in the sky and over every living creature that moves on the ground.' The power imbalance is reinforced by the fact that humans alone are made 'in God's image' and so share God's transcendence over the lower ranks of existence. Remembering the historical importance of religion to Western worldviews, it is hard to avoid the suspicion that God's gift of domination over nature helps explain its subsequent mistreatment.

Yet in non-religious traditions, our natural environment has fared no better. In the philosophical tradition from Aristotle to Descartes and beyond, human domination over nature is justified by the fact that humans alone are bestowed with the faculty of reason and so dictate the good of all. In the 17th century, combining religious and philosophical explanations for human mastery, Descartes declared that the God-given 'light of reason' distinguishes humans from all other living things. Humans rule over the natural world, he held, because humans are the only beings with a soul and hence the only beings with 'moral interests'.

Nor was the environment much better served by the sciences in the centuries thereafter. Here the prevailing worldview has been that the task of science is to understand the natural world as best we can, so as all the better to use it to humans' advantage. For all its merits, Charles Darwin's celebrated theory of evolution placed human existence at odds with the existence of all other species, in the great race of the 'survival of the fittest'. The success of humans over other species can thus be explained as in the natural order of things.

The principle that underlies and unifies these vast expanses of human thought is an ethical one. Ethics, we have noted, is the philosophical discipline which studies how humans should act. The principle that humans are the only beings whose interests are of concern to us in our theories of how we should act is thus an ethical principle. This principle is known as anthropocentrism, after the ancient Greek word for humans, *anthropos*. Anthropocentrism holds that humans are the only beings with a 'moral standing': that is, a *status* within our ethical theories. This principle was common across religion, philosophy and the sciences until the mid-20th century, when the consequences of maintaining it started to become apparent.

Thinking now about the many ways our environment is threatened by human actions on a global scale, we should surely challenge the ethical principles that have led us to this juncture. What reason, then, should we give for acting to protect our natural environment? Should we act because it is in *our own* best interests to do so – that of all humans, including the unborn? Or should we act because it is in the best interests of the *other* – non-human – beings affected by our actions? Should we act to protect our 'natural resources' or should we act to protect nature for its own sake? How should we act when these two alternatives do not align?

In the story of the good neighbour, the interests of the farmer and those of his neighbour are not at first in alignment: the farmer is happy with the shed he has built and the neighbour is not. Should the farmer agree to move his shed, then, because it is in his own interests or because it is in the interests of his neighbour. Should he act because he realises the consequences for him or the consequences for the neighbour of not doing so? Which of these is the better basis for action and why?

Arguments for protecting the environmental are often presented in terms of *our own* interests – and indeed, if saving the environment *is* in our interests, this appears a good reason to do so, all other things being equal. However, such reasoning reproduces the thinking which lies at the root of our environmental problems in the first place: anthropocentrism. It does not attribute a moral standing to non-human living beings in their own right. If it were discovered that some element of the environment did *not* benefit humans, for example, how should we respond? Are we entitled to wipe out mosquitos on this basis – or any other non-human living being we chose?

Should we defend the moral standing of non-human living things – and, if so, how? We might argue that non-human living beings have interests in just the same way humans do, interests that any reasonable ethical theory must address. Many animals are sentient: they have feelings and can suffer. An ethical theory that promotes happiness appears arbitrary if it promotes only the happiness of humans and not that of all living beings capable of happiness. Alternatively, we might argue that non-human living things have rights, just as humans do, and in this way extend moral standing to all living things, not merely those with sentience.

But does it make sense to say that animals and plants have rights, even though they cannot assert these rights in any meaningful way? Is it our duty to assert the rights of non-human beings for them – or is this simply to say, once again, that it is our place to decide the good of all? Again, in saying that non-human living beings have interests like our own, are we taking human interests as the model for what legitimate interests look like? Anthropocentric thinking seems harder to avoid than first appears.

It is very much a matter of debate in the field of environmental ethics whether it is possible to accord non-human living things the same moral standing as human in our ethical theories. What would be the consequences of such a principle? Presumably, vegetarianism would be foremost among them. How much further would we need to go, if *all* living things were to be respected?

Environmental ethicists who reject anthropomorphism tend to do so from a holistic metaphysical standpoint – that is, they argue that humans co-exist with other living things, each a small part of the larger natural environment as a whole. Humans have no particular priority, nor even significance, within this environment. There is no distinct property that entitles a human to a moral standing in any way different from that of any other living being. The English environmentalist James Lovelock, for example, saw the world as a single organism, a huge and complex living being, which must be addressed by our ethical theories in its entirety.

Adopting this approach, what might we say of the farmer in our story? In visiting the underground house of his neighbour, we might say, the farmer came to understand that his neighbours were part of his world, just as he was part of theirs, and that both were part of a world shared with all the other living beings around them. The farmer gave his neighbours the respect they deserved, we might say, not because they were somehow related to him as persons, but rather, because he recognised them as fellow beings, living side-by-side with him, another curious participant in that great wonder of this planet we call 'life'.

CHAPTER NINE

JOHN OF THE TUFT

Many years ago, in a far-off realm, there lived a queen who had, unknowingly, provoked the anger of a powerful witch. The queen's insult to the witch was unintended, but felt no less keenly for all that, with the result that the witch did not bestow her blessings on the birth of the queen's first-born son. The son was born ugly, to the point where the queen's attendants looked at him with horror and turned their heads.

The queen was distraught. 'Is there no way you can make the child prettier?' she pleaded with the witch. So passionate was she that the witch was at last persuaded to show mercy. She announced that the young prince's ugliness would be balanced by gentle manners and keen intelligence. What is more, he would have the power to bestow upon whomever he loved the same gentle manners and keen intelligence.

The queen was mildly reassured. She named her son John and, because he was born with a single tuft of hair on his head, he was known as John of the Tuft.

Shortly afterwards, in a neighbouring realm, a second queen was due to give birth to twins. The witch happened to attend this birth as well. When the first daughter was born, she was as beautiful and radiant as the sun. The queen was so exuberant about the child's beauty that it was feared she might endanger the second, as yet unborn, twin. So the witch dampened the queen's mood by announcing that the first daughter would be every bit as foolish as she was beautiful. When that did not do the trick, the witch added that the second daughter would be ugly.

The queen was distraught, not so much at the thought of the first child's foolishness as the thought of the second child's ugliness. 'Is there no way you can make the child prettier?' she pleaded with the witch.

'I can do nothing for her, Your Majesty,' the witch replied. 'But do not concern yourself. I'll bestow upon the child such intelligence that her lack of beauty will hardly be noticed.' And then, recalling her promise to John of the Tuft, she added, 'And the first child shall also be compensated: she shall have the power to bestow upon whomever she loves the same beauty and radiance as she possesses.'

As the princesses grew up, their perfections grew in them. Everyone marvelled at the radiance of the older princess, the beautiful Bella, and the wit of the younger, the clever Prudence. It is true that their flaws grew in proportion to their perfections, so that Bella grew sillier by the day while Prudence grew plainer, but that was hardly noticed.

At a certain point, as is common among princes and princesses, the time arrived for the queens to contemplate their children's marriages. Portraits of the young princesses were sent far and wide, in the hope of securing advantageous alliances. The portrait of the older princess provoked quite a stir, as you may well imagine.

There is surely little doubt that beauty confers great advantages on the young. Despite this evident fact, the younger princess proved to be more successful in society than the older. People would naturally go first to Bella, to admire her and compliment her on her loveliness. But then, equally naturally, they would soon turn to Prudence, to converse with her on a thousand interesting and entertaining things. The older princess could not fail to notice this. Without the slightest regret, would have given all her beauty to have but half her sister's wit.

One day, escaping the court and walking in nearby woods to reflect on her misfortune, young Bella saw approaching a most unusual-looking young man. He really was extraordinarily ugly, but he was superbly dressed and presented himself so politely that the princess was careful to show respect. This, of course, was John of the Tuft, who had fallen for the princess on seeing her portrait and had come to seek her affections.

Overjoyed to find the beautiful princess alone, he greeted her with the best manners possible. Yet he plainly observed that the princess was distracted and sorrowful. So, after they had conversed politely for a while, he said, 'I cannot comprehend how a person of such beauty can be as sorrowful as you appear to be. I can boast of seeing many beautiful women, but none as radiant as you.'

'I hope it pleases you to say so,' replied Bella, but said no more.

'Beauty,' continued John of the Tuft, 'is such an advantage, it surpasses all else. Since you possess this to the utmost degree, I can see nothing that could much affect you or lead to sadness.'

'I had far rather,' cried Bella, losing her reserve, 'be as ugly as you and have the good sense you possess, than have the beauty I possess and be as stupid as I am.'

John took surprisingly little offence and replied as amiably as he knew how: 'There is nothing that shows greater good sense than to believe you have none. It is in its very nature that, the more we have of it, the more we want. And this is so, for the beautiful and the ugly alike.'

'I would not know about that,' replied the princess wistfully. 'All I know is that I am stupid and wish not to be.'

'If that is all that troubles you, Princess, I can put an end to your sadness.'

'And how might you do that?'

'I have the power to give to the person I love as much good sense as can be had. Since you are that person, it will be your fault alone if you refuse this gift … provided that you might in time be so gracious as to agree to marry me.'

Young Bella was quite confused by this and did not know what to say, so she said nothing, which of course showed remarkable good sense.

'I do not wonder at your confusion, Princess, so I will give you some time to think it over. Let us return to this place in one year and agree to marry then.'

The princess had such a longing for good sense that she could not imagine going another year without it. So she agreed to meet John in one year's time and to marry him, should they both be so inclined. She was surprised, more than anything, that someone of such obvious wit and intelligence would be interested in marrying someone as stupid as herself.

No sooner had Bella agreed to marry him, however, than she discovered she had an incredible facility for expressing whatever was on her mind in a polite, easy and natural manner that was formerly foreign to her. She began at that moment a spirited conversation, which she kept up at such a rate that John suspected he had given her more wit than he had reserved for himself.

When she returned to the palace, the courtiers did not know what to make of her astonishing transformation. They now heard as many clever phrases and sensible observations as they had formerly heard absurdities. In the weeks that followed, Bella started to hold counsel in her apartments, inviting all the great minds of the realm. The queen herself started taking her older daughter's advice. Prudence alone was unimpressed.

The news of Bella's transformation travelled far and wide and many a young prince arrived at the palace, seeking to gain her favour. She found that none of them had sense enough for her. She reflected fondly on her conversation with John of the Tuft and wondered why no-one else appeared quite so witty.

After some time, however, there came a young prince who was so handsome, so rich, so powerful and so witty that she could not help feeling inclined towards him. His conversation sizzled; his observations were acute; his thoughts were deep and cryptic; his mind was like a steel trap, which aimed to capture everything inside it. And if, as Bella vaguely suspected, he did believe himself so much cleverer than she, then why did he court her so insistently? Being now sensible, Bella took time to consider his proposal of marriage.

One day, in an uncertain frame of mind, Bella went by chance to the wood where she had met John of the Tuft some time before. She was walking in profound meditation when she heard a great confusion of noise, as if a multitude of people were running backwards and forwards among the trees. Listening more closely, she heard: 'Bring me that pot!' and 'Quick, stir the gravy!' and 'Take care with that cake!'

Bella entered a clearing in the forest and stumbled upon an army of cooks and helpers preparing a banquet and setting up great tables for some splendid entertainment. Astonished at the sight, Bella enquired what was going on and for whom the entertainment was being prepared.

'Why, for Prince John of the Tuft,' came the reply. 'He is to be married tomorrow!'

The princess was more surprised than ever, until she recalled all at once that it was now twelve months since she had promised to marry the prince. She had forgotten her promise because, when she made it, she had been very foolish. Her promise was like much else she had put to the back of her mind from those earlier days.

She had not travelled many steps further when she came across John of the Tuft himself, magnificently dressed, like someone who was about to be wed.

He rejoiced on seeing her. 'I knew you would come!' he exclaimed, beaming.

Bella was thrown into a state of extreme confusion: 'You do know,' she insisted, 'that I was a fool when I promised to marry you. If you sincerely wished to make me your wife, you'd have done better to preserve my stupidity, rather than make me see things more clearly than I did before.'

'I know nothing of the sort,' replied John of the Tuft. 'Is it reasonable that a man of good sense should be *less* able to win your love when you share these very same qualities?' This stopped Bella in her tracks, as well it might.

'But let us get to the point,' he continued. 'If it were not for my ugliness, is there anything else about me that would displease you?'

'No, not at all,' Bella admitted.

'Then it is within your power to make me the most amiable of men,' John observed. In the year since he had last seen Bella, he had sought the advice of the witch, who had informed him of the promise she had made to Bella at birth. 'If you love me enough to wish it were so, you too could bestow upon me the gift of beauty, just as I bestowed upon you the gift of good sense.'

'If that be so, then I wish with all my heart that you be the most appealing of men,' Bella declared. The princess had no sooner pronounced these words than John of the Tuft appeared to her as the most handsome and lovable man in all the world.

Now there are those who might observe that Bella's transformation occurred at the very moment when John of the Tuft acknowledged her good sense. And they might equally observe that John's transformation occurred at the very moment when Bella admitted her love for him, despite his ugliness. Some might say that the princess needed her intelligence recognised by someone she respected before she could see it in herself. And perhaps, having reflected on the numerous good qualities of the young prince, the princess no longer saw the ugliness of his face or body: the squint of his eyes seemed now to concentrate their brilliance; his great red nose now appeared grand and heroic; his uneven limbs now gave him a gentle swaying gait which charmed her.

However that may be, these transformations did indeed take place. There was doubtless something extraordinary about them, but that may have had more to do with the magic of love than with any magic a witch was ever able to weave. And so the marriage feast of Bella and John of the Tuft took place in fairy tale fashion, there in the forest the following day, according to the instructions that the groom had given to his army of cooks and helpers many months previously.

WHAT DO YOU THINK?
QUESTIONS TO PONDER

Is it true that beauty confers great advantages on the young? Are these greater than the advantages of intelligence, do you think?

Can we say what beauty consists in? Are there some properties which are objectively beautiful? Or is it true — as often claimed — that beauty is in the eye of the beholder?

If you had to decide between beauty and wisdom, which would you choose and why?

PHILOSOPHICAL CONUNDRUMS: WHAT IS BEAUTY? WHAT IS LOVE?

This story is one of the lesser known from the collection *The Tales of Mother Goose* by the great French writer and collector of fairy tales, Charles Perrault, a collection which includes *The Sleeping Beauty, Cinderella, Puss in Boots* and *Little Red Riding Hood*. The story has been updated, but echoes the original in outline and themes. Foremost among these themes is the relative value of beauty and reason. The story is unusual among fairy takes in failing to give undisputed priority to a princess's beauty: Bella is clearly better served by any good sense she may have than by her beauty.

The relative value of beauty and reason is a theme as old as literature itself. Consider the story of Paris, who was silly enough to admit his preference for the beauty of Aphrodite over the wisdom of Athena. Athena had the last word, unsurprisingly. When Aphrodite rewarded Paris by giving him Helen – supposedly the most beautiful of mortal women – he was so overcome by her beauty that he captured her, took her to Troy and thereby unleashed the torrent of bloodshed of the Trojan War, in which he was himself was slaughtered.

Modern readers are often surprised by the undisputed status given to beauty in these ancient sources – and indeed, the idea that Paris should be so overcome by Helen's beauty as to lose his reason was initially unquestioned. Beauty was considered an objective and undeniable quality of a thing or a person, with a power so great as to start wars. It is most certainly not in the eye of the beholder, as Shakespeare was later to propose.

Philosophy has worked hard to overturn Paris' judgement of the relative importance of reason and beauty. Drawing attention to his mentor Socrates' ugliness – he reportedly had an unfortunately large head, bulbous eyes and prominent nose – Plato nevertheless proclaimed him the best and most noble of men. His beauty was held to lie in the inner quality of wisdom. Socrates, Plato insisted, was never swayed by external beauty – a property of the body – but always remained true to the inner life of reason – a property of the mind.

Plato did not challenge the ancient worldview entirely, however, for he did not deny that beauty and reason exist in a state of conflict. Nor did he deny that beauty is an objective quality of the beautiful thing itself, rather than merely something *we* see in that thing. Again, beauty lies in its possessor, not in its beholder.

If beauty does indeed lie in the thing itself, then it seems reasonable to ask: what exactly does beauty lie in? If beauty is an objective property of a beautiful thing, we might surely ask: what property is that? Many alternative candidates have been proposed: harmony, integrity, perfection and purity are clearly amongst the noticeable qualities of a beautiful thing. But then a further question arises: how exactly are these abstract qualities expressed in an object, so as to make one thing beautiful and another less so?

What makes us value the Mona Lisa over other paintings, for example? Why is this painting the foremost example of beauty in art: its subject, the way it is painted, its proportions, its colours, its tone? Is it possible, for example, to delineate the exact proportions that lead us to find this painting more beautiful than others?

Here at least, by contrast with other questions of definition we have considered in this volume, we appear to have an agreed example of the quality we are trying to define. Yet the property of beauty in the Mona Lisa may be as elusive as her smile. For, while people may agree that the painting is beautiful, they will likely disagree about what it is about that painting that makes it so. Nor are they likely to agree on the properties this painting has in common with a beautiful sunset or a beautiful vase of flowers – or a beautiful poem, for that matter.

How serious a problem is this? Should we all agree on questions of beauty? We all have experience of disagreeing with others on what looks good to us, or of suddenly seeing the beauty of something where previously we had not. Considering how widespread are such experiences, we may be inclined to admit that beauty lies entirely in the eye of the beholder.

The great advantage of this approach is that an object's beauty is then in principle measurable: it can be measured by how many people consider the object to be beautiful or by the degree to which people find it beautiful or some calculation of the two. But is it reasonable to make our concept of beauty entirely relativistic? Should something as culturally significant as beauty lie entirely in the court of the public opinion? Does this approach subject beauty to the fickleness of human taste?

Returning to our story, some philosophers have noted in recent years that – oddly enough – there are gender issues implicit in the discussion of beauty. From the Greek myths onward, it is the beauty of women that leads men like Paris to irrational acts which cause wars: only a woman's face could 'launch a thousand ships' – warships, that is – as Helen's is supposed to have done. To the modern reader, this suggests that the possession of beauty is not always the boon it is supposed to be. Bella's story suggests the same.

It may be, however, that Bella's beauty is a disadvantage to her, not so much in itself, but because the possession of beauty and the possession of reason are treated as being somehow at odds. By contrasting beauty and reason – Bella and Prudence – this story initially presents the two in the traditional way, as if they exist in conflict. Knowing no better, Bella sees herself the way others see her and believes that, because all anyone sees is her beauty, it is the only virtue she possesses. When John of the Tuft suggests that good sense is its own virtue, which has nothing whatsoever to do with beauty or ugliness, she sees the reason in what he says. Her shift in understanding is transformative, like other transformations we have seen in this volume.

This brings us to a further theme in this story, which concerns love. John, it appears, loves Bella on sight. Is this even possible? Bella, in turn, appears to make a decision to give her heart to John. Is love something to be decided in this way? The indefinable quality of love raises questions related to those of beauty. What does love consist in? Does it involve seeing beauty in the beloved? If so, does it involve losing one's reason in the beloved's presence, as does beauty? Although this is a popular conception of love, the examples of Bella and of John of the Tuft suggests a more measured approach.

What, then, is love? Does it consist in valuing the beloved over others, respecting their finest qualities, desiring to be with them more than others? Might love take different forms, depending on the lover and the beloved, or on the nature of the relationship between them or the context in which they find themselves? If so, how do we define what these various forms of love have in common? Here, once again, the question form 'What is …?' raises a plethora of further questions.

If philosophers have been suspicious of beauty, so much greater is their suspicion of love. Socrates proclaimed romantic love to be a misplaced response to physical beauty, as opposed to the higher form of beauty that pertains to the mind. Descartes justified his certain knowledge of his own existence by claiming that, at that moment he was thinking, he existed as a 'thinking being' and nothing else: 'I think, therefore I am'. As is traditional, Descartes held both sensations and emotions to be naturally untrustworthy and liable to lead him astray. Reason, on the contrary, provided the foundation for all else he might know. Was he right in this, do you think? Could the same result have been achieved by appealing to his certainty in the possession of an emotion? Does 'I love, therefore I am' work as well?

Chapter Ten

Heracles' Thirteenth Labour

Heracles, son of the god Zeus, was perhaps the greatest of the Greek heroes. He is known for accomplishing twelve heroic labours, for which Zeus had promised him the gift of immortality. Yet there is one further labour – we might call it a thirteenth labour – that is not included in the official legends told of this hero. This may be because it shows Heracles in a less decisive frame of mind, by contrast with the shrewd determination he displayed in killing the many-headed monster, the Hydra, or stealing the belt of Hyppolite, Queen of the Amazons.

The story goes like this. Heracles had just completed his fifth labour, which was to clean out the stables of the King Augeas. The task was particularly difficult and unpleasant because, being both divine and immortal, the stables' cows produced immense quantities of dung. Heracles accomplished the task by diverting two nearby rivers to flow through the stables and so rinse it clean. Yet the uncompromising Eurystheus, who devised these labours, was unimpressed. Declaring that the stables had been cleaned by the surging rivers rather than by Heracles himself, he added further tasks to the list.

Heracles' next tasks were to save the people of Greece from flocks of man-eating birds and to save the people of Crete from a thunderous bull which was rampaging through the countryside, causing devastation. Travelling westwards, Heracles located the murderous flock, drove the birds into the air with a rattle given to him by Athena for the purpose, and shot them down, one by one. Then, pleased with the relative ease of this sixth labour, Heracles set sail for Crete.

The island of Crete lies off the Greek mainland, in the placid Mediterranean Sea. Its King, Minos, had received the bull as a gift from the god Poseidon, but then failed to sacrifice it as promised to the god, and it ran amok. He was pleased, therefore, that Heracles had come to sort things out for him. Minos, as we shall see, would later gain fame in the story of the Minotaur, a half-man, half-bull, who would in time devastate the people of Athens, just as its father, the Cretan Bull, was doing in Crete. But that is another story. For the moment, our focus is on the Cretan Bull, which Heracles sought to capture.

Heracles soon discovered that his task would not be as easy as he had expected, even for one as heroic as he. Although the bull was a huge creature, it was it difficult to locate. The plain of destruction the animal wreaked was so vast and the devastation so total that it was difficult to tell where the beast had come from or where it was headed. The mountainous terrain across the island meant that there were plenty of places for the beast to lurk. So, on arrival, Heracles he had no clear idea where he should go, nor how he should complete his mission.

Now, unfortunately for Heracles, the relations between the Cretans and the Greeks at the time were not neighbourly. Heracles clearly marked himself out as Greek by his armour, his bearing and by the companions travelling with him, all dressed with care in current Grecian style. Heracles was the son of Zeus, who had come to Crete precisely to prove his birthright. It would have done him no favours, he believed, to pretend to be less than he was. None of this warmed him to the local population, however, since it was known to the Cretans that the Greeks viewed them with contempt.

To be a Cretan, said the Greeks, was to be a liar and a scoundrel. No doubt few Greeks had ever met a Cretan and their beliefs were simple bigotry, but Heracles guessed the real cause: when the Greeks Thetis and Medea argued over who was the more beautiful, they gave the task of deciding between them to Idomeneus, a man who happened to be from Crete. When Idomeneus proclaimed Thetis the more beautiful, the sorceress Medea screamed that he was a liar and cursed the Cretans never to tell the truth.

Whatever the effect of Medea's curse, the Cretans' knowledge of the Greeks' low opinion of them may cast light on Heracles discussion with a ragged traveller, a lowly wanderer, the first local he came upon and questioned about the bull.

'Ah, so it's the bull that you're after, is it?' the wanderer mused. 'Well, as to that, I can give you an answer, fair and square.'

'I'd thank you for your advice,' gestured the hero with uncharacteristic humility, admitting his ignorance of Crete.

'I'm a Cretan, through and through, so I should know what I'm talking about,' assured the wanderer, who described in detail the direction Heracles should take and the terrain he would encounter. 'You must head through the mountains towards Knossos,' he insisted.

Thanking him, Heracles was about to head off in that very direction when the wanderer stopped him: 'But there's one further thing you should know before you proceed,' he said, the twitch of a smile on his lips.

'What's that?' asked Heracles, curious.

'Cretans always lie.' And with that, the man turned and walked away.

Heracles stood for a moment watching the man's back, wondering whether he had just made himself the butt of some obscure joke. At first, he felt inclined to dismiss the Cretan's words as mere nonsense. Yet something bothered him. What did the man mean? Did he mean he was lying? Should he take the path the man suggested or should he go in a different direction altogether? But if he were lying about the direction Heracles should take, was he also lying in everything else he had said? Did he even know the Cretan landscape? Was he even from Crete at all?

But then, what about his claim that Cretans always lie? Was he also lying then? If his claim were true, it would mean that he, a Cretan, always lied and so must be lying when he said that as well. But if he was lying, that would mean that he was in fact telling the truth – the truth, that is, that Cretans lie. In other words, if he was telling the truth, it would follow that he was lying, and yet, if he was lying, it would follow that he was telling the truth. What was going on here?

Slowly, the gravity of the problem the Cretan had given him dawned on Heracles and, as it did, the effect of finding himself bested by a ragged wanderer began to take its toll. Doubt about the correct course of action did not came naturally to Heracles. He was a man who was inclined to fight first and ask questions later. To doubt himself was deeply discomforting. Yet it appeared to be the only option available.

Is this where Medea's curse had inevitably led, Heracles wondered idly. Could he in fact trust any single thing a Cretan had to say? Were the Greeks right in judging the Cretans to be liars and scoundrels … but if they were, did that mean that the wanderer was honest after all? As the Cretan's three words spun around in his head, Heracles felt himself going in circles. As far as he could see, the only sensible course of action was to put the riddle out of his mind and follow the wanderer's directions, in the hope that their truth or falsehood might in time be revealed.

After some hours of hiking through the countryside, Heracles came to a village where the local people were busy going about their daily business. He approached a group of farming men to ask about the whereabouts of the bull. They were friendly and welcoming, and keen to provide him with the information he needed. The answers he received gave him no comfort at all.

One man declared with total conviction that the bull must be north-east, since the path of destruction clearly lead in that direction. Another challenged this, saying that it was obvious to anyone with eyes that the bull must by now be due east. Yet another declared with equal force that the evidence suggested that the bull was to the south-east. Given his location on the west coast of Crete, the only other alternative was that the bull was south, so it hardly surprised Heracles when a fourth young man came forward to claim that option as his own.

Evidence of the bull having been in the neighbourhood was widespread, though there was no evidence of the actual presence of a bull – or none that Heracles could see. Then a further thought hit him: what evidence was there of a bull on Crete at all? His belief in the bull was based on the claims of the people of Crete. But if Cretans aways lie, how could he know that the bull even existed? Perhaps what he took to be evidence of the existence of a bull was evidence of something else entirely. Whereas earlier he felt vertigo, now he felt the ground falling away beneath him entirely.

Heracles was soon asking himself about the point of speaking to anyone at all on the island, given that anything they said could be refuted by three small words. Even if he received a response from a Cretan that turned out to be true, it would do nothing to show they hadn't lied to him. The speaker may have *accidentally* told the truth. Heracles had no access to other people's thoughts. He had no way of knowing whether Cretans always lied or were the most honest souls in all Zeus' kingdom. Why bother with them at all?

But then again, were Cretans so different from any other people? Heracles had always trusted in the honesty and wisdom of the Greeks, but now he started to doubt even them. It seemed obvious enough that notions of honesty and wisdom rely on notions of truth. To believe that someone is honest and wise is to believe that their claims are true – true, that is, *and not false*. Yet now, Heracles had to admit, he wondered whether the relationship between true and false was as clear-cut as he used to think.

As Heracles left the village and ventured onwards, his mind started to race. In the absence of better alternatives, he determined to follow the path the wanderer had proposed, both physically and intellectually. So it was not long before another thought occurred to him: what was he to say to someone who declared, in all honesty, 'This sentence is false'? If the sentence were true, then it must be false. And if the sentence were false, then it must be true. Heracles was disgusted … it was happening all over again.

How could a simple sentence be true and false at the same time? Heracles rebelled against the idea of it with every fibre of his very substantial being. It defied everything his mother had taught him about the wisdom of common sense: that a true sentence is obviously not false and a false sentence is obviously not true. If you could not believe in that, Heracles wanted to know, what *could* you believe in? What is left of truth and honesty and wisdom and all those values that, as a good Greek citizen, he held dear?

'It makes no *sense!*' Heracles bellowed into the Cretan mountains, as he bore down upon them angrily. So loud were his words that they roused the Cretan Bull, which was curious to see who was stomping through its territory with such fury in his voice. And Heracles was so riled, so furious with the Cretans for having challenged and confused him, that he was in no mood to be messed with.

* * *

It is doubtless the mark of a great mind to trust the judgement of none but itself. Whatever his assessment of the honesty of the Cretans he met on his travels, mythological sources record the success of Heracles' mission to defeat the Cretan Bull, capturing it and returning with it to the tyrant Eurystheus on the Grecian mainland. Thus Crete was liberated from its terrorising bull and Heracles was left to accomplish the remaining five labours in the wake of his success. The story is by no means over, since it remained for Theseus, foremost among the next generation of Greek heroes, to overcome the offspring of the Cretan Bull, the dreaded Minotaur.

At one level at least, we know that Heracles attained the immortality promised to him by Zeus for completing his twelve labours. To anyone even slightly familiar with Greek philosophy, it will come as no surprise that he was more successful in these than in his thirteenth labour, to resolve the famed 'liar's paradox'. Some philosophers believe that the liar's paradox remains unresolved, even after the lives of those who first grappled with it have passed into legend. And this suggests that sometimes intellectual labours are even more challenging than physical labours – and are, perhaps, the most challenging of all.

What do you think?
Questions to ponder

What is the problem with declaring: 'I am now lying' or 'This sentence is false'? Can you explain the problem to someone who has never heard of such paradoxes?

Must a statement be either true or false? Could it be both true and false at the same time? Under what circumstances?

Is it true that intellectual challenges are more difficult than physical ones?

PHILOSOPHICAL CONUNDRUMS:
WHAT'S WRONG WITH A PARADOX?

The story of Heracles meeting the Cretan wanderer and encountering the liar's paradox is not canonical. It is not told in the classic of the 8th century BC, the *Iliad* of Homer, nor in the other ancient sources where we read of the life of the legendary hero. I nevertheless include it here to draw attention to the importance of logic in our study of philosophy. The story of the defeat of the Cretan Bull *is* canonical, by contrast, as is the story of Medea's curse upon the Cretans.

The liar's paradox is also ancient. That said, when it first appeared, the 'Cretan liar' was not treated as a paradox at all. When, in around the year 600 BC, the Cretan Epimenides claimed that 'all Cretans lie', he allowed the possibility that sometimes, at least, Cretans tell the truth. The problem was merely to tell when a Cretan was lying and when they were telling the truth. The formulation in this story – 'Cretans always lie' – was proposed later, to underline the paradox in what the Cretan had said.

Paradoxes such as this are encountered in the field of logic. Logic is the branch of philosophy which studies the structure of reasoning, to identify the rules which govern sound argument. In logic, a paradox is a statement or set of statements which, while appearing innocuous, are either contradictory in themselves or lead to contradiction. Paradoxes appear to show that the reasoning that leads to the contradiction must be invalid. The difficulty then lies in identifying precisely where the mistake is.

Outside the confines of logic, paradoxes are also often found in the thought experiments of modern literature and film, such as the time paradox in *Back to the Future*, where the time traveller must somehow ensure the marriage of his parents, so that he himself may one day be born. We also speak of paradoxes more broadly as statements which are unexpected or ironic, as when CS Lewis dedicated *The Lion, the Witch and the Wardrobe* to his goddaughter with the words, 'some day you will be old enough to start reading fairy tales again'.

Time paradoxes are the speciality of a philosopher from the 5th century BC, Zeno of Elea. A good example is the 'Achilles paradox', which shows that, if the Greek hero Achilles gives a tortoise a head start in a running race, he will never be able to catch up with it and will inevitably lose the race. For, by the time Achilles reaches the point at which the tortoise started, the tortoise will have moved on and reached a further point. Then, by the time Achilles reaches that further point, the tortoise will have moved on further again. And so on, indefinitely. Achilles can never overtake the tortoise, despite the fact that he was greatest of all the Greek warriors and hero of the Trojan War.

We have already come across a well-known paradox in Chapter 2, in claim attributed to Socrates: 'All that I know is that I know nothing'. The paradox here is that, if it is true that Socrates knows nothing, then clearly he knows *something*, which undermines his original claim to know *nothing*. If it is false that Socrates knows nothing, on the other hand, then again he knows something, but what he knows – *nothing* – undermines his original claim to know *something*. Socrates' claim takes the standard form of this kind of paradox: if it is true, then it must be false and, if it is false, then it must be true.

Like the liar's paradox, this is paradox of self-reference. These paradoxes arise when a statement includes itself within the field of statements it applies to. There are numerous paradoxes of this nature, including the 'omnipotence paradox', which challenges God's claim to be – as God is commonly defined to be – all-powerful. The question that leads to the paradox is this: is it possible for God to create a stone so heavy that he himself is unable to lift it? Whatever answer we give, God is apparently not omnipotent. The paradox is sometimes supposed to undermine the entire concept of God, at least as traditionally understood.

Another example was invented in the early 20th century by the English philosopher, Bertrand Russell. Russell gave the example of a town barber: this barber shaves the heads of all the men of a village who do not shave themselves. All looks fine with this formulation until we ask: does this barber shave himself? If he belongs to the group of people who do not shave themselves, then it follows from the formulation of the problem that he does indeed shave himself. If, however, he belongs to the group of people who do shave themselves, then it follows that he does not. And so, this paradoxical barber both does and does not shave himself.

What is the problem with paradoxes? For many, they are an appealing intellectual puzzle. For logicians, however, paradoxes challenge the principles underlying our structures of thought: the principle that a statement cannot be *both* true and false at the same time (the so-called law of non-contradiction) and the principle that every statement must be *either* true or false (the so-called law of the excluded middle). These are basic laws of logic, upon which our notions of reason are based. What happens when such laws are challenged? Could they collapse? Would the entire structure of our knowledge then collapse as well? This is the possibility that so riled Heracles in the story. Unfortunately, the solutions to the problem of paradoxes are notoriously technical and well beyond the scope of this discussion. They sometimes involve an appeal to logical 'metalanguages', where the statement that a claim is true is considered to stand at a different logical level from the words of the claim itself. We shall leave the details to the logicians to try to sort out.

What is within this scope of this discussion is the point that none of the proposed solutions to the problem of paradoxes has yet received universal acclaim. This is not the first time we have noticed that philosophical problems steadfastly resist resolution. We may not find this so surprising in the fields of ethics or religion perhaps. That it should happen in logic, the discipline we expect to furnish us with the principles governing thought, may tell us something about the fragility of truth itself.

CHAPTER ELEVEN

THE SHIP OF THESEUS

There was once a time, in the early days of ancient Greece, when the powerful King Minos of Crete made war on the people of Athens. He came with a great fleet of ships and a huge army, and devastated the villages and fields around Athens. Then he set up camp around the city walls and sent word to Aegus, the King of Athens, that the following day he would march his army into the city, slay the people, burn the houses and destroy the Temple of Athena, the crown of Athens sitting atop the Acropolis.

With his elders, King Aegus went out to Minos to try to reason with him. Minos was in no mood to negotiate. His son had been ambushed and murdered by a band of Athenians — or so he believed — and Minos intended to avenge his son's death. 'The Athenians have robbed me of my dearest treasure,' he declared, 'and I demand of Athens its dearest treasure in return.' And so he outlined his demand: 'Every seven years, the Athenians must choose seven young men and seven young women from amongst its finest, who will sail to Crete in tribute to me.'

'What will become of these young people?' asked the King fearfully.

'They will be fed to the Minotaur.'

Aegus wept. The Minotaur was a huge and terrifying monster, half-man and half-bull, which lived in the Labyrinth, an enormous palace that had to be built especially to house the beast. So large and elaborate was this palace that those who entered it were soon lost. None were ever seen again. Aegus could not bring himself to agree to such a frightful settlement, but the elders were pragmatic: 'It is better that a few should perish than that a whole city should be destroyed,' they argued.

So the shameful treaty was reached between the two kings and the tributes began. Every seventh year, when the roses bloomed and the doves twittered, the finest youth of Athens were placed on a black-sailed ship and sailed to Crete to pay tribute as King Minos required. As each of these years approached, the Athenians begged their protector, the goddess Athena, to end to the carnage. 'How long can this go on?' they wept.

* * *

Meanwhile, in a small Greek village far from Athens, a child by the name of Theseus was growing into manhood. His father was King Aegeus, who had returned to Athens when the war with Crete had broken out and no longer even knew whether his son was dead or alive. When Theseus reached his twentieth birthday, he determined to journey to Athens to announce himself to his father and claim his inheritance.

Within weeks of setting out, the name of Theseus was being acclaimed across the plains of Greece. For Theseus used his journey to perform a series of truly heroic feats and so set the scene for what was to come: at each of six entrances to the underworld, he saved the local people from murderers, robbers and torturers, subjecting each to the same treatment they had meted out to their victims. As word of Theseus' deeds reached Athens, in advance of his arrival, the Athenians were thrilled that such a heroic young man should have arrived in time to replace their king, who was rapidly ageing under the stress of his subjugation to the Cretan king.

The day of his arrival in Athens was not propitious, however, since it happened to be the day on which the young Athenians were chosen as tributes to be sent to King Minos on Crete. As Theseus made his way to his father's palace, the doors in every street were shut and the streets deserted. Everyone shut themselves inside, silent and fearful, dreading to hear whose lot it was to be fed to the Minotaur.

Making his way to the palace of his father and announcing himself, Theseus insisted on knowing the reason for the strange behaviour of the Athenians. 'What is the meaning of this?' demanded Theseus, when the situation was explained to him. 'What right has a Cretan to demand tribute from Athens?'

'Let us speak no more of it,' said Aegus, repeating the advice of his elders: 'It is better that a few should die, than that Athens itself should be destroyed.'

'Of course we will speak no more of it,' Theseus replied, 'for I do not intend to let it go on any longer.' He had determined that he himself would travel to Crete, along with the other young men and women of Athens, to slay the Minotaur in its home, the Labyrinth.

Now Aegus wept all the more. Theseus had only just been returned to him and did not wish to lose him again. 'You are the hope of Athens. You cannot offer yourself up to the monster,' he cried, desperate to avoid the calamity he saw unfolding before his eyes.

'If I am the hope of Athens, I can do nothing else,' was all Theseus could reply. He refused to discuss the matter further or to rethink his plans. So, when the black-sailed ship departed for Athens some days later, Theseus stood at its helm.

* * *

The ship of Theseus made good progress on the fair spring winds across the Mediterranean and soon landed in Crete, just as the hero Heracles had done years earlier in his pursuit of the Cretan Bull, the Minotaur's father. As the ship landed, the young men and women were taken by Cretan soldiers and paraded through the streets in a show of submission to King Minos. This was their final indignity, in advance of being taken to the Labyrinth the following day.

When they reached the palace gate, King Minos himself greeted them, his daughter, the princess Ariadne, at his side. 'What fine young tributes!' Minos gloated.

'Yes, Father, far too fine to be fodder for the vile Minotaur,' Ariadne rebuked him. Looking at the young man who led the Athenian tributes, she knew she had never seen anyone so fine. For the rest of the day and the night, she grieved that Theseus and his companions should perish so senselessly. At first light, she decided to act.

She hurried to the prison where Theseus was held. Into his hands she delivered a knife that could be used to slay the Minotaur and a skein of silk thread which could be fastened to the door of the Labyrinth and unravelled as the Athenians passed through its twisting passageways. In that way, the Athenians would be able to retrace their steps to the entrance of the palace and would not find themselves hopelessly lost once the Minotaur had been slain.

The following day, the Athenians were led into the Labyrinth and shut within it. For hours they wandered, waiting for the moment when the beast would set itself upon them. They prayed to all the gods for their safety, though the prayers of Theseus were reserved for Apollo, the god who showed particular care for the young. Before he had set sail, many an Athenians had commented on his resemblance to the god.

Late in the evening, the Minotaur finally emerged from a labyrinthine passage, roaring and raging. He was twice the size of a man and his head was like that of a bull, with sharp horns, fiery eyes and huge teeth. When he saw Theseus with a dagger in his hand racing forward to meet him, he paused, for no-one had ever dared face him with such clear determination. Head down, horns forward, the bull charged. But Theseus timed his strides and caught hold of the bull's horns as it reached him, vaulting over the bull's head and then using the bull's momentum to hurl himself over its monstrous back. As he passed, he gored the beast's neck with his dagger.

The Minotaur fell to the ground, groaning and beating the dirt with his hoof-like fists. Deftly, Theseus retraced his steps, plunging the dagger into the monster's heart before it had the chance to raise itself. The Athenians barely had time to recover their shock at the speed with which the deed was done, before Theseus was guiding them out of the Labyrinth, following the path of thread he had attached to the door on entering. Through a thousand winding ways they passed, until they reached the entrance and found Ariadne waiting nervously to free them and return with them to their ship.

It took some time for King Minos to realise that, because of his cruelty, the second of his treasures, his daughter Ariadne, had also been lost to him. By the time the truth hit him, Ariadne and the Athenians were far out to sea and steering towards Athens. On the way, however, they stopped at Delos, the most sacred of all the Mediterranean islands and the birthplace of Apollo, to thank the god for their deliverance and offer him a tribute of meats, honey, wine and milk.

* * *

Now, the Athenians were naturally overwhelmed with gratitude to Theseus and to the god who had helped him slay the Minotaur. To show their thanks, it was decided that the ship on which Theseus had sailed should now plot a new course. Each year, the ship would set sail to pay tribute to a much worthier recipient than in the past: the god Apollo, on the island of Delos, who had protected the young people of Athens. Over the years, this tradition was maintained, as a symbol of Athenian prestige and favour amongst the gods. And indeed, as the years passed, Athens steadily rose to power and came to dominate the entire Mediterranean Sea.

As with any ship, then as now, the shipbuilders had their work cut out for them, keeping the ship of Theseus afloat. The ship was made of wood and so was of course liable to rot. Before a beam had become rotten to the point of endangering its voyage, it had to be replaced with a new one. In this way, over the decades, the beams of Theseus's ship were replaced by the shipbuilders in Athens, until at last the day arrived when there was no longer a single beam of the ship that had carried Theseus on his original passage to glory.

It may be true that the ancient Athenians were philosophers at heart. How else can we explain the flowering of philosophy in Athens during these centuries? And perhaps this was helped by the fact that, in the Athenian forum, the philosophers would meet and converse and take money from wealthy young citizens, in exchange for their teaching in philosophy.

One day, a debate broke out among the young philosophers who met in the Athenian forum: each challenged the other to prove that the ship docked in the harbour was indeed the ship of Theseus. This was no idle question amongst them, but a matter of the proper veneration of the god Apollo, whom all young Athenians pledged to honour. For them, Theseus' boat was the link between themselves and their hero, their bond to the god who had protected him. Tradition demanded that the Athenians preserve this ship, to venerate the god Apollo, for just as long as time allowed.

Was the ship in the harbour the true ship of Theseus? How could it be, some argued, given that it no longer contained a single beam of the original ship? The philosophers who argued thus were well-read: some repeated Heraclitus' claim that you can never step into the same river twice, since the waters of that river are constantly being replaced. Others rejected this argument in the name of common sense: Heraclitus himself could not deny that the ship had sailed to Delos every year since Theseus' original visit, so how could he dispute the ship's authenticity now? At what point, exactly, had it stopped being Theseus' ship?

Thus the argument raged, one half of the marketplace arguing that it was of course the ship of Theseus, since every beam of it had been carefully replaced with an identical one, and the other half arguing that the fact that every beam had been replaced showed that it was not the ship of Theseus at all.

Then something happened which challenged the young philosophers still further. For a wealthy merchant by the name of Aristos chose this moment to announce that the beams of Theseus' original ship still existed. Going back several generations, Aristos' family had realised the value of the beams, given their association with the hero and with his god. One by one, as they were replaced, the family had bought the beams from the shipbuilders. More with an eye to their own well-being than that of Athenian tradition, the family had carefully treated the beams so that they would remain seaworthy.

Thus Aristos had come by the beams of original ship of Theseus and had made a new ship, an exact replica of the original, using the very same beams. This ship was now on the market. The ship that lay in the harbour, he claimed, was not the true ship of Theseus. His own ship had a greater claim, since it was made not merely of the same design, but also of the same material substance, as the original.

Unfortunately for Aristos, he did not live to discover whether his claim was accepted by the Athenians, nor to enjoy the wealth he expected as a result. On the day Aristos' ship put out to sea to prove its seaworthiness, a plank from the ship's stern fell on Aristos and killed him. It was widely assumed that Aristos had lost favour with the gods for his scheming and reaped the inevitable reward. Such is fate. Inevitably also, the incident was held to weaken his ship's claim to be the true ship of Theseus.

History does not relate what happened to the ships of Theseus. In time, both ships rotted and became unseaworthy and could no longer be used to honour Apollo in the traditional manner. Another legendary Greek ship – the *Argo* – was saved from oblivion by being hurled skywards by the sea god Poseidon and so lives on as a constellation sailing the Milky Way, protecting the sailors who have used it for navigation ever since. But the *Argo* is merely an exception in the great, sweeping tide of time. As the centuries passed, even the Greek gods themselves ceased to be, replaced by a more powerful god. Nevertheless, the tales of the people who believed in these ancient gods live on and their philosophies do not cease to inspire.

WHAT DO YOU THINK?
QUESTIONS TO PONDER

Which is the true ship of Theseus: the ship with its beams replaced gradually over time or the ship constructed later, from the original beams? They cannot both be, surely?

Given that everything in this world is always changing, is it fair to say that we can never step into the same river twice?

Given that every cell of a human body is replaced over time, does it follow that that, when we age, we are no longer the same person as when we were young? If we are the same person, what is it, exactly, that preserves our identity?

PHILOSOPHICAL CONUNDRUMS: WHAT ULTIMATELY EXISTS?

The legend of Theseus and the Minotaur, like that of Heracles, dates back as far as the 8th century BC, to Homer's *Iliad*. The thought experiment called 'the ship of Theseus' is younger: it was mentioned in the 1st century by Plutarch, who noted that philosophers were at that time equally divided on the question of whether Theseus' ship remained the same or not, once its beams were fully replaced. The question whether the ship's replacement, built from the original design and beams, was the same ship was introduced in the 17th century by the English philosopher, Thomas Hobbes.

The questions of identity raised by the 'Ship of Theseus Problem' are serious concerns for philosophy, touching on fundamental questions of the nature of reality. They include relatively mundane questions, such as when I ask whether the axe I inherited from my grandfather is still the same axe he used, once its handle and blade have been replaced many times over. They extend to questions which affect our sense of self, such as when we ask whether a person is still the same person, once every cell of their body has been replaced many times over or, more seriously, their mind has been transformed in some fundamental way. We want of course to be able to say that the amnesia or the stroke victim is the same person as before, but there are difficulties.

To explain these, let's consider the ship of Theseus. Let's call Theseus' original ship, Ship A. Let's call the ship with all its beams gradually replaced, Ship B. And let's call the new ship built from the beams of Theseus' original ship, Ship C. Now, a fundamental law of logic dictates that, for any A, if A is identical to B and A is identical to C, then it follows that B is identical to C.

Here, then, let's allow that Theseus' original Ship A is identical with Ship B, because Ship B has been constructed by the gradual replacement of Ship A's parts. Let's also allow that Theseus' original Ship A is identical with Ship C, because Ship C has been constructed on the same design directly from Ship A's parts. If we allow both of these, however, then it follows that Ship B and Ship C are identical: one and the same. But this is clearly not the case, since the two ships are in two distinct locations and have different histories. What's gone wrong with this analysis?

Another example clarifies the issue. Let's imagine it's not a ship, but a human, whose parts are being replaced. Imagine firstly that, in a great feat of medicine, every part of your body is replaced over time as it starts to fail. Now imagine, secondly, that an evil surgeon takes all the removed body parts, rejuvenates them somehow and then uses them to create a new human being. Which one of them is *you*: the one whose body parts were replaced slowly by degrees or the one reconstructed from your original body parts? It is not difficult to see that they cannot both be. But which is the real you?

The 6th century BC Greek philosopher Heraclitus, mentioned in this story, is reported to have claimed that there is no identity in this world, since all is flux. The river metaphor is his: if the river were not constantly in flux, it would no longer be a river, but something more like a lake or a pool. And so it follows: you cannot step into the same river twice. Whatever we think of the metaphor, it does seem reasonable and in accordance with our experience to note that change is a fundamental feature of the world.

What does this mean for the identity of the things we take to survive across time? Does it mean that there is no identity, since identity implies the existence of something that endures through time? Or does it mean that the identity of a thing may lie in the changes it undergoes? If so, does this imply that constancy and change are not opposed, as we normally take them to be? It is not surprising that this philosopher was nicknamed 'Heraclitus the Obscure' for his efforts in explaining this last point.

This returns us to the questions raised about existence in Chapter 5 and Plato's claim that the things of this world – the things that come into being and pass away – cannot be said definitively to exist. These things cannot truly exist, according to Plato, since otherwise what is true at one moment would be false at the next.

Truth cannot be capricious in this way. Truth relates to what is constant and existence must therefore belong to what is eternal and unchanging.

Plato theorised that there must exist a higher world — an immutable realm — from which the things we see around us — the mutable things — derive their reality. He called this the world of 'Forms', by contrast with the world of 'Appearance'. He understood the Forms to be like an abstract template to which the things of this world correspond or an essence in which they participate. The world of Forms cannot be seen or experienced with the senses, but it can be intuited with the intellect. The philosopher's training consists in identifying these Forms, whose existence resolves the problems of identity created by a world of endless change. Does it, do you think?

The differing approaches of Heraclitus and Plato to questions of identity mark out two important trends in a field of philosophy called metaphysics. Metaphysics, we have noted, is the study of the fundamental questions of existence. It asks the deepest and most profound questions of philosophy: what is being? What truly exists? What is ultimately real? It asks questions so perplexing that it's hard even to know where to start with them: what meaning is there in existence? Why is there something rather than nothing?

We have come across metaphysical questions throughout this volume: does God exist? Is there such a thing as luck or fate? Must existence be physical or do imaginary beings exist? Do human beings and non-human living beings share existence as part of larger living being, the natural world? We have seen how our answers to these metaphysical questions shape other areas of philosophy and we have glimpsed the fact that their influence spreads outward: to the arts, the sciences and indeed all fields of human understanding. Some metaphysicians would say that our answers to metaphysical questions provide the foundations of understanding itself.

Before finishing, let me draw attention to the elders' claim that the Athenian youth must be sacrificed for the sake of the greater good, the preservation of Athens. The dilemma facing these Athenians takes a form of a well-known problem in philosophy, named the 'Trolley Problem'. This ethical problem invites you to imagine that a tram (or 'trolley') is careering along a track where a group of labourers is working, who will be killed if you do not pull a switch to divert the tram to another track, where there is a single worker. Should you pull the switch and make yourself responsible for the death of the single worker, or should you do nothing, leaving natural forces to decide the fate of the group of labourers? Should the one – or the few – be sacrificed for the many?

Theseus is surely justified in refusing either of these options, but then he is a hero of ancient literature and so not bound by the usual constraints. For most of us, deciding the outcome for the poor tramline labourers is a more stressful exercise. They are no doubt subject to the capricious nature of fate, discussed in Chapter 6. That same force may also be at work in the downfall of Aristos, which echoes that of the fabled Greek seafarer Jason, killed by a beam of his boat, the *Argo*, before it was sent to journey across the Milky Way.

One last version of the Ship of Theseus problem also deserves mention here, because it provides an excellent overview of the many philosophical issues that have been raised in this volume. This version has been named 'Neurath's boat' after the Austrian philosopher, Otto Neurath, who likened the situation of philosophers to that of the makers of Theseus' ship. Philosophers, he said:

> are like sailors who in the open sea must construct their ship but are never able to start afresh from the bottom. Where a beam is taken away, a new one must at once be put there, and for this the rest of the ship is used as support. In this way, by using the old beams and driftwood, the ship can be shaped entirely anew, but only by gradual reconstruction.

In this manner, the identity of philosophy is preserved for those who follow. If you enjoyed this book and happen to be thinking in terms of a future profession, why not think of adding a beam or two to Neurath's ship, as it sails so intrepidly across open seas?

SOURCES

The stories in this volume are not in their original forms. They have been abridged, updated and changed in other ways to suit their purpose in introducing issues of philosophical interest to a contemporary audience. Names, language and small elements of plot have been changed where appropriate. In outline and themes, however, most remain largely as in the original. The stories of Chapters 4, 10 and 11 are my own dramatization of ideas taken from source materials below.

Chapter 1:   HC Andersen, 'The Goblin and the Huckster' in *What the Moon Saw and Other Tales*, George Routledge and Sons, London, 1866.

Chapter 2:   Katharine Pyle, 'Dame Pridgett and the Fairies', in *Tales of Folk and Fairies*, Little, Brown and Co., Boston, 1919.

Chapter 3:   Katharine Pyle 'The Dreamer' in *Fairy Tales from Far And Near*, Little, Brown and Co., Boston, 1922.

Chapter 4:   The idea of the invisible gardener found in John Wisdom, 'Gods', *Proceedings of the Aristotelian Society*, Vol. 45, 1944-45.

Chapter 5:   Anatole France, *Putois*, PF Collier and Son, New York, 1907.

Chapter 6:   Howard Pyle, 'Hans Hecklemann's Luck' in *Pepper and Salt*, EM Hale and Co, Eau Claire, 1886.

Chapter 7:   Howard Pyle, 'The Apple of Contentment' in *Pepper and Salt*, EM Hale and Co, Eau Claire, 1886.

Chapter 8:   'The Neighbour Underground' in Clara Stroebe (ed), *The Norwegian Fairy Book*, Frederick A Stokes Co, New York, 1922.

Chapter 9:   Charles Perrault, 'Riquet with the Tuft' in *The Fairy Tales of Charles Perrault*, George G Harrap and Co, London, 1922. First published as *Stories or Tales from Times Past; or Tales of Mother Goose*, 1697.

Chapter 10:   The story of Heracles is found in many ancient sources, including Euripides' *Heracles* (5th century BC) and Ovid's *Metamorphoses* (1st century).

Chapter 11:   The story of Theseus and the Minotaur is found in many ancient sources, but prominent in Plutarch's *Life of Theseus* (1st century), which is also the source of the idea of the ship of Theseus identity problem. The version above, with some variations from Plutarch, borrows from James Baldwin, *Old Greek Stories*, American Book Co, New York, 1895. Hobbes' version of the ship of Theseus is found in *De Corpore*, 1655; Neurath's version is found in 'Anti-Spengler', 1921.

ABOUT THE AUTHOR

Victoria Barker holds a PhD in Philosophy and a PhD in
Studies in Religion, both from the University of Sydney,
and a PGCE from Kings College, London.
She has spent roughly thirty years teaching in universities and schools
in Sydney, Tokyo and London. She lives in Berlin.

www.ingramcontent.com/pod-product-compliance
Lightning Source LLC
Chambersburg PA
CBHW061432160726
47995CB00003B/861